Costumes for Nursery Tale Characters

Costumes for
Nursery Tale Characters

By

Jean Greenhowe

Photography by A.P.S. Aberdeen

Publishers   PLAYS, INC.   Boston

To my mother-in-law, Margaret Ann

Library of Congress Cataloging in Publication Data

Greenhowe, Jean.
    Costumes for nursery tale characters.

    British ed. (1975) published under title: Fancy dress from nursery tales.
    SUMMARY: Instructions with pictures and diagrams for making
costumes for fairy tale characters such as Robin Hood, Cinderella, Aladdin,
and Puss in Boots.
    1. Children – Costume – Juvenile literature. 2. Sewing – Juvenile
literature. (1. Costume) I. Aberdeen, A. P. S. II. Title.
TT560.G74 1976   792'.026   75-23444

ISBN 0-8238-0199-3

Printed in Great Britain

Contents

❧ *Acknowledgment* ❧

I wish to convey my sincere thanks to the following people.

The children who so enthusiastically modelled the costumes for the photographs in this book, Fiona, Grant, Morag, Patricia, Sean, Stephen and Victoria.

Mr George Ewen Smith, custodian of Provost Skene's House, Aberdeen, and Mr Ian McKenzie Smith, director of Aberdeen Art Gallery and Museum, for their kind co-operation and help in allowing some of the photographs to be taken in the period room settings of Provost Skene's House.

J.G.

✤ *Introduction* ✤

Most children love to play at dressing up, and every family toy box must surely contain a few old hats, dresses and shoes which provide hours of fun and amusement.

However, the occasion eventually arises when a special fancy dress is called for, and this can present quite a problem for those with little or no dressmaking experience.

In the following pages I have tried to show how to use simple pattern shapes to make a variety of costumes for children of about five to twelve years old, with a minimum of sewing. In some cases items of everyday clothing are incorporated into the fancy dress and only a couple of specially made garments are required to complete the outfit.

Most of the costumes are based on a very simple one piece tunic pattern which has only two seams. By cutting the tunic pattern longer or shorter and altering the sleeves and neckline, quite different garments can be produced to fit all sizes. I have also devised an easy way of making a fitted bodice with inset sleeves for the fairy godmother dress. Only straight strips of fabric are used and the bodice will fit any size of child. The theme of this book is Nursery Tale fancy dress, but the patterns and ideas for making the various garments should enable readers to design other costumes.

Full instructions are included for the accessories which identify some of the characters, and these are great fun to make from ordinary household objects and materials. A gravy boat is transformed into Aladdin's lamp and delicious looking hot cross buns can be created from nylon tights and felt stuffed with kapok!

Finally I have given some suggestions for dressing other Nursery Tale characters by varying and interchanging parts of the costumes in the book.

Apart from the reader who wishes to make individual fancy dresses, I hope that this book may be of some help to those faced with the problem of costuming a children's pantomime, pageant or play, when several outfits have to be made to fit children of different sizes.

❦ *General instructions* ❦

These should be read before starting to make any of the costumes.

Fabrics and other materials

The amounts quoted in the lists of materials required are sufficient to make costumes to fit children of about 142 cm (4 ft 8 in.) in height; not quite so much will be needed for smaller sizes. For those with very little dressmaking experience it would probably be safest to adhere to the amounts given even if the costume is for a smaller child. Any left over oddments could always be used up later on for dressing dolls or soft toy making. With the making up instructions there is no difficulty, since these are written to cover all sizes so that each garment can be made to fit any child's individual measurements.

Curtain fabrics are especially good for making fancy dress outfits since they are normally much wider than dress fabrics; this makes it possible to cut out some of the garments in one piece. Remnants of curtaining, usually too small for making curtains, can also be bought quite cheaply in the sales. The non-woven type of curtain fabric is useful because it is inexpensive and can be obtained in a range of bright colours. Very little finishing off is required on garments made from this fabric, since the raw edges do not fray. Cheap curtain brocades look very rich when used for fancy dress, but because the raw edges fray out rather easily a little extra care is needed when making up this type of fabric.

For waistband and other fastenings *Velcro* touch and close fastening is excellent, though hooks and eyes or snap fasteners can be used.

Stiff interlining is ideal for making firm hat and collar shapes and the stiffest kind of *Vilene* (*Pellon*) is best of all. This is sold for interlining curtain pelmets and home furnishing in general, and it is 82 cm (32 in.) in width. Thin card can be used as a substitute, but this, of course, will not stand up to ironing or washing.

As an economical substitute for ordinary braids, ribbons and trimmings, Christmas ribbon and gift wrapping braids can be used.

An old sheet, if available, will provide a valuable amount of fabric for making such things as underskirts, blouses and shirts.

Making the patterns and cutting out

The patterns should be drawn out to the measurements given on large sheets of brown

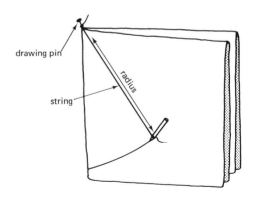

Drawing out large circles

wrapping paper. A long straight piece of wood is useful for drawing straight lines.

For many of the garments large circular patterns are required. To draw out a large circle, first fold a square of paper of sufficient size into quarters. Tie a pencil to one end of a length of string which should be longer than the required radius of the circle. Note that the radius of a circle is half the diameter. Measure the length of the radius along the string from the pencil and tie a knot in the string at this point. Place a drawing pin through the knot and into the folded corner of the square of paper. Now draw out a quarter circle, as shown in the diagram, keeping the string tightly stretched. Cut out, then open up the folded sheet to give the full circle.

Since the one piece tunic pattern is used in so many of the outfits it is a good idea to make the tunic from an oddment of fabric, such as old sheeting. This can then be tried on the child to see if any alterations may be necessary before cutting out the actual costume fabric. This can be especially useful when making several outfits for children of different sizes.

When a pattern is marked along one edge 'place to fold' this means to place the edge to a fold in the fabric, so that the pattern can be cut from double thickness to give a full sized garment.

The patterns for the Wolf's mask and the Frog Prince are given full size and they can be traced directly off the page.

Sewing and gluing

1·3 cm ($\frac{1}{2}$ in.) seams are allowed on all pieces unless otherwise stated. All seams should be pressed open after sewing.

Join all pieces of fabric with the right sides together unless other instructions are given.

In some cases glue is used for sticking fabric. This should be a contact adhesive such as *UHU*, which is colourless and dries very quickly.

❧ *The one piece tunic pattern* ❧

To draft out the tunic pattern use a sheet of brown wrapping paper measuring at least 66 cm × 96·5 cm (26 in. × 38 in.). Alternatively smaller sheets can be stuck together with sticky

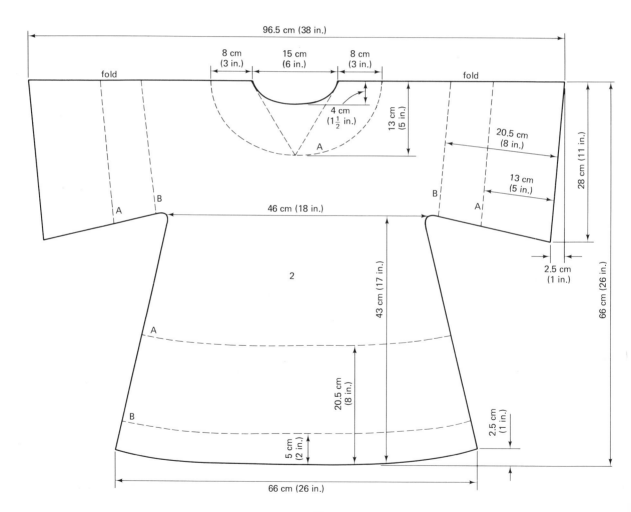

96.5 cm (38 in.)

8 cm (3 in.)   15 cm (6 in.)   8 cm (3 in.)

fold   fold

4 cm (1½ in.)

13 cm (5 in.)

20.5 cm (8 in.)

13 cm (5 in.)

28 cm (11 in.)

A   B   B   A

46 cm (18 in.)

2.5 cm (1 in.)

A   A

2

43 cm (17 in.)

66 cm (26 in.)

A

B

20.5 cm (8 in.)

2.5 cm (1 in.)

5 cm (2 in.)

66 cm (26 in.)

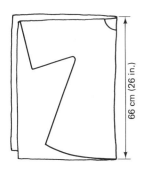

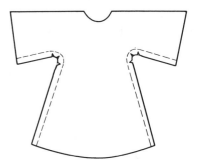

1 Showing the sheet of paper folded in half and the tunic pattern drawn on

66 cm (26 in.)

3 Cutting the tunic from double fabric placing the upper edge against the fold

4 Showing the side and underarm seams with clips in the underarm curves

tape to give the required size. Fold the sheet of paper in half as shown in diagram 1 and draw on the tunic to the sizes given in diagram 2, halving the measurements across the width of the pattern. Cut out the pattern, then mark on all the other lines shown on the tunic pattern.

When cutting out the tunic from fabric always place the top edge marked 'fold' to a fold in the fabric as shown in diagram 3. After sewing the underarm and side seams of the tunic, clip the fabric at the underarm curves as shown in diagram 4 so that the seams will not wrinkle when the tunic is turned right side out.

When the tunic hem edge or the sleeves have to be cut to a shorter length for a particular garment, the excess pieces can be cut off the pattern and laid aside. After cutting the tunic from fabric the pieces can be stuck back on to the pattern with sticky tape. In the same way extra length can be added on to the sleeve and hem edges.

The one piece pants pattern

Measurements are given for this pattern to be drawn out in three sizes. The smallest size is given first, then the medium and larger sizes follow in brackets. If in doubt about which size to use for the child, check the various measurements against a pair of ordinary trousers or pyjama pants which fit the child.

On a sheet of brown wrapping paper measuring at least 30·5 cm × 92 cm (12 in. × 36 in.) draw out the pants pattern to the measurements given in diagram 1. Cut out the pattern.

Cut out two pants pieces from fabric, each time placing the edge marked 'fold' against a fold in the fabric. Join the two pants pieces to each other at the centre edges as shown in diagram 2. Bring these seams together and join the inside leg seams as shown in diagram 3. Turn in and hem the ankle edges. Hem the waist edge, taking a 4 cm (1½ in.) turning to form a casing for the elastic. Thread the elastic through to fit the child's waist.

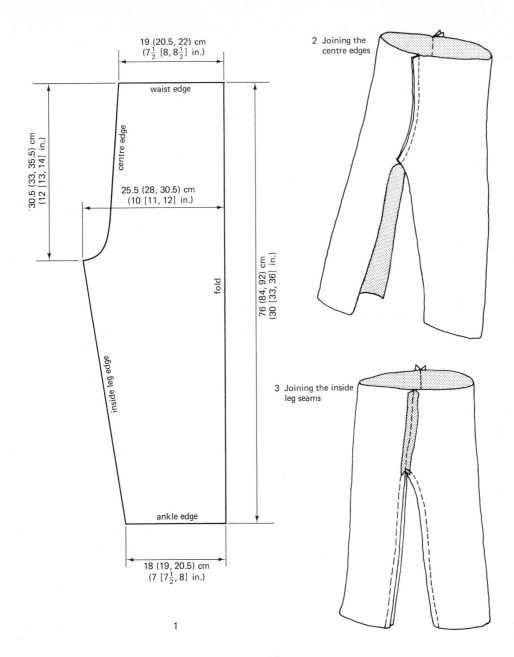

19 (20.5, 22) cm
($7\frac{1}{2}$ [8, $8\frac{1}{2}$] in.)

waist edge

centre edge

30.5 (33, 35.5) cm
(12 [13, 14] in.)

25.5 (28, 30.5) cm
(10 [11, 12] in.)

fold

76 (84, 92) cm
(30 [33, 36] in.)

inside leg edge

ankle edge

18 (19, 20.5) cm
(7 [$7\frac{1}{2}$, 8] in.)

1

2 Joining the
centre edges

3 Joining the inside
leg seams

Robin Hood and Friar Tuck

*Robin Hood and Friar Tuck made a plan to capture
the Sheriff of Nottingham's men*

Robin Hood

This is a quickly made fancy dress using green non-woven curtain fabric for the tunic and hood.

Tights and sweater

These can be green, brown or fawn.

Ankle boots

Use a pair of brown knee socks a few sizes larger than the child's foot. Turn the socks inside out and sew the toe ends to a pointed shape as shown in diagram 1. When turned right side out the socks can be worn on top of gym shoes or slippers, rolling the tops down around the ankles.

Tunic and hood

Materials required for height 142 cm (4 ft 8 in.)
1·4 m (1½ yd) of 122 cm (48 in.) wide green curtain fabric.
5.1 m (5½ yd) of plain braid for edging the tunic and hood; alternatively bias binding can be used.
    Two buttons and a shoe lace for the fastening on the hood.

To make the tunic
Use the tunic pattern given on page 10, shortening the sleeve and lower edges to the lines marked B. Place the pattern against the child to check that the hem edge comes slightly lower than the tops of the legs, then shorten or lengthen the pattern as necessary.

1 Sewing the toe ends of
the socks to a point

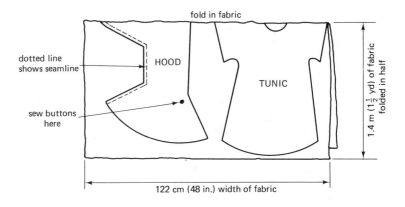

2 Cutting out the
tunic and hood

15

Cut the tunic from fabric as shown in diagram 2. Then cut out the V-neckline on the front of the tunic only, as shown on the tunic pattern. Join the underarm and side seams and clip the underarm curves. Try the tunic on the child to see if larger turnings need to be taken on these seams to make the tunic fit neatly. Sew braid or bias binding to the neck, sleeve and hem edges to cover the raw edges.

To make the hood
This hood will fit all sizes. Draw out the hood pattern as shown in diagram 3, beginning by drawing out a quarter circle with a 51 cm (20 in.) radius. Mark on the other dotted lines to the measurements given, then cut out the pattern. Cut the hood from fabric as shown in diagram 2 then join the back edges leaving the lower curved edge and the face edge open. Sew on braid or bias binding to cover these raw edges. Sew a button to each side of the hood at the neck line then make a small loop from the shoe lace and twist it around the buttons to fasten as illustrated.

Belt and quiver

Materials
A belt.
Small pieces of leather cloth and cardboard for the quiver.
Contact adhesive.

To make the quiver
Make the quiver pattern as shown in diagram 4 then cut out two pieces from leather cloth. Join the pieces together, taking 0·3 cm ($\frac{1}{8}$ in.) seam and leaving the top edges open. Turn right side out. To stiffen the quiver, cut two pieces of cardboard using the quiver pattern, then trim 0·6 cm ($\frac{1}{4}$ in.) off all the edges.

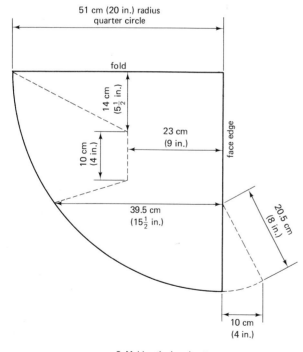

51 cm (20 in.) radius
quarter circle

fold

14 cm ($5\frac{1}{2}$ in.)

23 cm (9 in.)

10 cm (4 in.)

face edge

39.5 cm ($15\frac{1}{2}$ in.)

20.5 cm (8 in.)

10 cm (4 in.)

3 Making the hood pattern

Place the pieces of cardboard inside the quiver, one at the front and one at the back. Then fold the top edges of the leather cloth to the inside and glue to the cardboard.

Cut 1·3 cm ($\frac{1}{2}$ in.) wide strips of leather cloth and glue these around the quiver as shown in diagram 4. Sew two loops of leather cloth to the back of the quiver to hang it on the belt as illustrated.

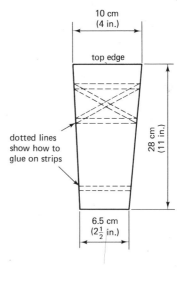

4 The quiver

Bow and arrows

Use a toy bow and arrows.

⤚⤙ *Friar Tuck* ⤚⤙

This costume is quick and easy to make using non-woven brown curtain fabric. To give Friar Tuck the necessary stoutness of figure, a couple of extra sweaters or an anorak should be worn underneath the tunic. A small circle of pink felt moulded to shape is used for the tonsure, the bald patch on the head, and this can be fixed to the child's hair with hair grips.

Tunic and collar

Materials required for height 142 cm (4 ft 8 in.)
2·8 m (3 yd) of 122 cm (48 in.) wide brown non-woven curtain fabric.
46 cm ($\frac{1}{2}$ yd) of narrow elastic.

To make the tunic
Use the tunic pattern given on page 10, lengthening the sleeve edges to make full length sleeves, and lengthening the hem edge so that it will reach to the child's ankles. A little extra should also be allowed on the side and underarm seams to give more fullness if the tunic is for an older child.

Cut the tunic from fabric as shown in diagram 1. The sleeve edges can be taken to the full width of the fabric, and this extra can be folded back if the sleeves are too long for the child, as shown in the illustration. Cut out the rounded neck edge a little lower than given on the tunic pattern.

Join the underarm and side seams and clip the underarm curves. Clip the neck edge at intervals, then hem the neck, sleeve and lower edges.

To make the collar
Draw out the collar pattern as shown in diagram 2. This collar will fit all sizes. Cut two collar pieces from fabric as shown in diagram 1, then join the pieces at the sides leaving the top and lower edges open. Hem the top and lower edges, then thread elastic through the top edge to draw it in slightly. When the collar is worn, turn the top edge to the inside, forming folds as shown in the illustration.

Girdle

For the girdle use 1·9 m (2 yd) of very thick cotton piping cord. This can be dyed brown.

Sandals

Any kind of strap sandals can be used. Alternatively, to make the sandals as shown in the illustration, cheap plastic flip-flop sandals are used. Remove the toe straps and replace them with long brown boot laces, lacing these around the feet and ankles as shown in the illustration.

Tonsure

For this use a 15 cm (6 in.) diameter circle of pink felt. Soak it thoroughly in a strong solution of starch, then ease it over the base or the inside of a small pottery bowl to give the correct shape to fit the child's head. Allow to dry, placing the bowl in a warm oven if desired to speed up the drying process. When the felt is dry, glue four short lengths of tape inside the circle close to the outer edge, leaving a gap at the centre of each tape unglued through which a hair grip can be slipped, as shown in diagram 3.

Stick

Friar Tuck carries a stout stick. For this a suitable straight branch cut from a tree can be used, or a length of wooden dowelling.

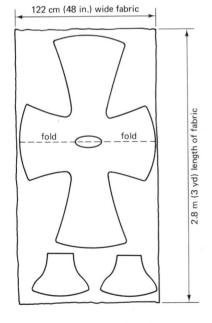

1 Cutting out the tunic and hood pieces

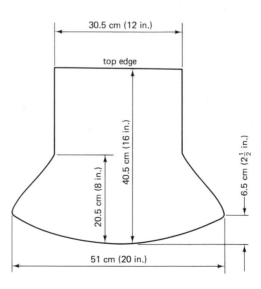

2 The collar pattern

3 Showing how to fix the tapes inside the tonsure

Little Miss Muffet sat on a tuffet,
Eating her curds and whey; there came a big spider,
Who sat down beside her and frightened Miss Muffet away.

ᨒ᨞ᨒ *Little Miss Muffet* ᨒ᨞ᨒ

This outfit is made from thin curtain fabrics, using flower printed nylon for the dress and hat, and plain coloured net with frilled edges for the shawl top and lower sleeves. A long nightdress could be used instead of making the dress; then only the shawl top, hat and spider would have to be specially made.

Dress and hat

Materials required for height 142 cm (4 ft 8 in.)
3·2 m (3½ yd) of 92 cm (36 in.) wide printed nylon curtain fabric.
2·8 m (3 yd) of 92 cm (36 in.) wide fabric for lining the dress, or cuttings from an old sheet.
46 cm (½ yd) of 82 cm (32 in.) wide stiff inter-lining for the hat brim.
1·6 m (1¾ yd) of 92 cm (36 in.) wide plain net fabric with ready frilled edges.
92 cm (1 yd) of 5 cm (2 in.) wide ribbon for the belt.
46 cm (½ yd) of narrow ribbon in the same colour as the belt.
5 cm (2 in.) of *Velcro* for the belt fastening, or hooks and eyes can be used instead.
56 cm (22 in.) length of narrow elastic.
Contact adhesive.

To make the dress
Use the tunic pattern given on page 10, altering it as follows: shorten the sleeve edges to the lines marked A, then cut out the neck edge along the line marked A. Lengthen the hem edge of the pattern so that the tunic is just above ankle length on the child. The pattern width requires no alteration as the belt, gathered sleeve

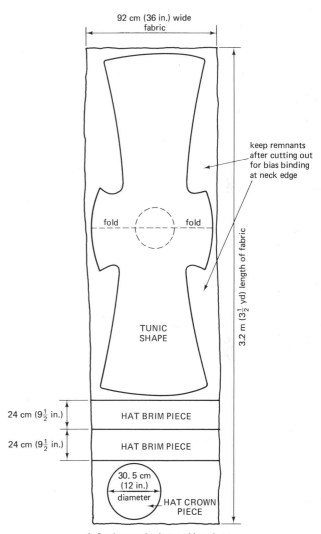

92 cm (36 in.) wide fabric

keep remnants after cutting out for bias binding at neck edge

fold   fold

3.2 m (3½ yd) length of fabric

TUNIC SHAPE

24 cm (9½ in.)   HAT BRIM PIECE

24 cm (9½ in.)   HAT BRIM PIECE

30. 5 cm (12 in.) diameter   HAT CROWN PIECE

1 Cutting out the dress and hat pieces

21

edges and elasticated neck edge ensure that the dress will fit all sizes.

Cut out the tunic shape and hat pieces from printed fabric as shown in diagram 1. Join the side and underarm seams of the dress then clip the underarm curves. Hem the lower edge, then turn the dress right side out. Cut out the tunic shape from the lining fabric, join the underarm and side seams in the same way as for the dress, then hem the lower edge. Turn the lining right side out and place it inside the dress. Tack the raw neck and sleeve edges of the lining and dress together, then bind the neck edge with bias strips of dress fabric and thread the narrow elastic through.

Cut out the pieces from the frilled edged net fabric as shown in diagram 2. To make the lower sleeves, pin each of the sleeve pieces right side inside around the child's arms as shown in diagram 3, having the 30·5 cm (12 in.) length of the fabric along the length of the arms, and pinning the fabric loosely enough so that the sleeves can be pulled off the arms easily. Pull the sleeves off and sew the seams as pinned then trim off the excess fabric close to the seams.

Gather the raw sleeve edges of the dress to fit the upper raw edges of the plain net sleeves, then stitch them in place.

Cut the ribbon for the belt to the child's chest size just beneath the arms, plus 2·5 cm (1 in.) for an overlap. Sew the *Velcro* or hooks and eyes to the overlap.

For the shawl top, fold the 92 cm (1 yd)

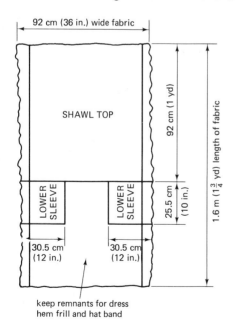

2 Cutting out the frilled edged net pieces

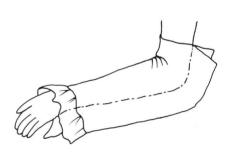

3 Pinning the sleeve fabric to fit around the arm

length of plain net fabric in half, bringing the two frilled edges together. Tie a length of strong thread tightly around the centre of the strip as shown in diagram 4 and pin this tied centre to the outside of the belt at the centre front. Place the belt on the child, then take each side of the shawl piece back over each shoulder. Gather up each end of the shawl piece and pin inside the belt on either side of the overlap fastening. Sew the ends in place where they are pinned. Now run a gathering thread through the fabric along each shoulder, drawing up the gathers as necessary to make the shawl top fit on the shoulders as shown in the illustration. Fasten off the gathering threads. Make a bow from the narrow ribbon and sew it to the centre front as illustrated.

Make a frill from strips of the remaining plain net fabric and sew the frill to the dress hem.

To make the hat

For the hat brim, cut out two 40·5 cm (16 in.) diameter circles from the piece of interlining, then from the centre of each one cut out an 18 cm (7 in.) diameter circle and discard it. Cut a section out of each brim shape as shown in diagram 5. Glue the two brim pieces together around the edges.

To cover the brim join the two 24 cm × 92 cm (9½ in. × 36 in.) pieces of dress fabric together to make a 24 cm × 184 cm (9½ in. × 72 in.) length. Fold this strip in half along the length with right sides outside, then stitch the long edges together, taking 0·6 cm (¼ in.) seam. Slip this tube of fabric on to the brim shape, with the seam at the inner edge of the brim. Space out the pleats of fabric evenly. Overlap the short edges of the brim shape 0·6 cm (¼ in.) and stitch, then turn in the remaining short raw edges of the tube of fabric and slip stitch them together so that the brim is completely covered.

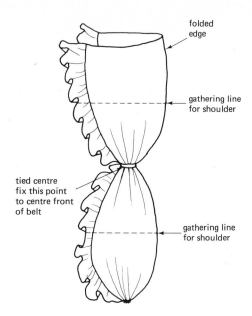

4 Showing shawl top folded in half with one end gathered

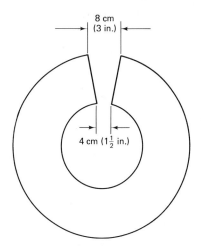

5 Cutting a section out of the brim shape

For the crown of the hat use the 30·5 cm (12 in.) diameter circle of dress fabric and also cut out a 30·5 cm (12 in.) diameter circle of lining fabric. Place the pieces together with the right sides uppermost, then run a gathering thread round the edge through both thicknesses. Pull up the gathers so that the crown will fit the inner edge of the brim. Sew the crown in place, taking 0·6 cm ($\frac{1}{4}$ in.) seam and spacing out the gathers in the crown evenly. Cut a strip of the left-over plain net fabric and tie it round the hat for a hat band, holding it in position with a stitch here and there.

Shoes and socks

Ballet shoes or slippers can be worn with coloured socks to match the dress fabric.

Bowl and spoon

Use a plastic bowl and spoon in a colour which matches the dress fabric.

The spider

Materials
Small piece of brown velvet or felt for the body.
Scrap of white felt and two sequins for the eyes.
Cotton wool for stuffing.
Length of wool or thin string for the legs.
Contact adhesive.

To make
Cut a 9 cm ($3\frac{1}{2}$ in.) diameter circle of velvet or felt and run a gathering thread around the edge. Put a little stuffing in the centre of the circle and

pull up the gathers slightly. Continue adding more stuffing until the body is a firm rounded shape. Pull the gathering thread tight and fasten off. This gathered side is the underside of the spider.

Cut two ovals of white felt for the eyes, measuring about 0·9 cm × 1·6 cm ($\frac{3}{8}$ in. × $\frac{5}{8}$ in.) Glue these in position, then glue on sequins as shown in diagram 6.

For the legs cut four 11·5 cm ($4\frac{1}{2}$ in.) lengths of wool or string. Using a darning needle take each length through from one side of the body to the other, spacing them out evenly and leaving equal lengths of wool protruding at each side to form eight legs. Spread glue on all the legs, allow it to become tacky, then bend the legs into shape as shown in diagram 6.

6 Showing positions of legs on spider

For the spider's thread use a short length of silvery thread if possible, taking it through from the underside of the spider to the top of the head with a darning needle. Tie a knot in the end of the thread underneath the body and attach the other end of the thread to the edge of the hat brim, as shown in the illustration.

Cinderella brought a pumpkin and six small mice,
then the Fairy Godmother waved her magic wand . . .

❧ *Cinderella* ❧

Cinderella's cage of six small mice and the pumpkin make this an attractive outfit though it costs very little to make. Instructions are given here for the blouse and skirt, but a child's ordinary blouse and an adult's old cotton skirt could be used instead.

Skirt

Materials required to fit any size
Two strips of 92 cm (36 in.) wide cotton fabric the required length from waist to ankles.
A length of petersham ribbon about 2·5 cm (1 in.) wide, the child's waist measurement plus 8 cm (3 in.), for the waistband.
Velcro or hooks and eyes for the waistband fastening.
Scraps of bright printed fabrics for the patches.

To make
Machine stitch fabric patches all over the skirt pieces as shown in the illustration. Join the strips of skirt fabric at the sides, leaving a 15 cm (6 in.) gap at the top of one seam for the side opening. Gather up the waist edge to fit the child's waist and sew it to the length of ribbon. Sew *Velcro* or hooks and eyes to the waistband at the overlap. Cut the lower edge of the skirt in to ragged points.

Blouse

Note that this blouse will fit all sizes because of the elasticated sleeve and neck edges.

Materials
92 cm (1 yd) of 82 cm (36 in.) wide brushed nylon fabric.
92 cm (1 yd) of narrow elastic.

To make
Use the tunic pattern given on page 10. Shorten the lower and sleeve edges to the lines marked A, then cut out the neck edge along the line marked A. Cut the blouse from the fabric.

Hem the sleeve and neck edges forming casings for the elastic. Thread elastic through the sleeve edges to fit the child's upper arms and sew the ends of the elastic in place at the ends of the casings. Thread elastic through the neck edge to fit as illustrated.

Join the side and underarm seams, then clip the underarm curves. Hem the lower edge.

Belt

Materials
A 10 cm (4 in.) wide strip of felt long enough to go around the child's waist.
A strip of stiff interlining the same size as the felt.
A long boot lace.

To make
Stitch the felt and interlining together all round about 1·3 cm (½ in.) from the edges. Trim a little off the edge of the interlining so that it will not show on the right side of the belt. Snip five small holes at even intervals in each of the short edges of the belt. Thread the boot lace through as shown in the illustration.

Scarf

Use a man's handkerchief.

Shoes

Cinderella can have bare feet, or wear gym shoes or slippers.

Cage of mice

Materials
A small lampshade frame. The one illustrated measures 11·5 cm (4½ in.) diameter at the narrow end, 14 cm (5½ in.) diameter at the other end by 11·5 cm (4½ in.) in height. It has six struts.
String, for making extra struts on the cage.
Small piece of card for the cage base.
Brown enamel paint.
Scraps of fleecy fabric or felt for the mice.
Cotton wool for stuffing.
Small black beads for eyes.
Pink felt for ears.
Yellow *Plasticine* for the lump of cheese.
Contact adhesive.

To make
First remove any lamp fittings from the lampshade frame. Fill in the gaps between the struts and across the top by tying on lengths of string, keeping the string taut. Make a string loop at the top of the cage with which to carry it. Paint the entire cage with enamel paint and put it aside to dry.

Cut a circle of card to fit the bottom of the cage. Model the *Plasticine* into a wedge shape and make round holes and scooped-out bits as though nibbled by the mice. Glue the cheese to the card base.

For the mouse pattern use one quarter of a 10 cm (4 in.) diameter circle of paper. Cut out six mice from fleecy fabric or felt. Oversew the straight edges of each mouse piece together, turn right side out and stuff with a little cotton wool. Run a gathering thread round the remaining raw edge and pull up tightly, enclosing one end of a bit of string for a tail. Fasten off the thread.

Glue two tiny beads to each head for eyes about 1·3 cm ($\frac{1}{2}$ in.) from the pointed end. Mark the pointed end with black pen or pencil for the nose. Make the whiskers by taking a needle and double black thread through the face just behind the nose, then snipping the threads short on either side of the nose.

For the ears, cut 0·9 cm ($\frac{3}{8}$ in.) diameter circles of pink felt. Cut a small straight edge off each one and stick these edges in position behind the eyes.

Glue all the mice to the cage base around the cheese in various positions, as shown in the illustration. Then glue the edge of the base to the lower edge of the cage.

Pumpkin

Materials
A strip of yellow fabric 23 cm × 61 cm (9 in. × 24 in.).
Kapok for stuffing.
Small piece of green felt for the pumpkin stalk.
Strong nylon or other thread for tying around the pumpkin.
Contact adhesive.

To make
Join the 23 cm (9 in.) edges of the fabric strip, then gather up one of the remaining raw edges tightly and fasten off the thread. Turn right side out and stuff firmly. Gather up the remaining raw edge and fasten off the thread. The gathered edges form the top and base of the pumpkin.

To form the pumpkin 'sections', tie threads very tightly around the pumpkin, crossing them over at the top and base as shown in the illustration.

For the stalk cut a 5 cm × 9 cm (2 in. × 3$\frac{1}{2}$ in.) strip of green felt; snip one 9 cm (3$\frac{1}{2}$ in.) edge into points. Spread the strip with glue and roll it up along the length spreading out the points to glue to the top gathered point of the pumpkin. Glue stalk in place.

For a more realistic effect, paint streaks of green, white and yellow water paint on the pumpkin.

❧ The Fairy Godmother ❧

This costume could also be used for Cinderella in her ball dress or any other fairy tale princess.

Dress and hat

Materials required for height 142 cm (4 ft 8 in.)
3 m (3¼ yd) of 122 cm (48 in.) wide shiny curtain fabric.
4·4 m (4¾ yd) of silver braid or trimming.
2·3 m (2½ yd) of 92 cm (36 in.) wide transparent non-fray fabric or fine curtain net.
70 cm (¾ yd) of narrow elastic.
3·7 m (4 yd) of nylon ribbon.
Hooks and eyes or snap fasteners for the bodice fastening.
A 35·5 cm (14 in.) square of stiff interlining for making the hat shape.
Small strip of *Velcro* for the wrist band fastenings.
Contact adhesive.

To make the dress
First make the bodice. Cut a strip of curtain fabric 25·5 cm (10 in.) wide, long enough to go around the child's chest plus 11·5 cm (4½ in.). Turn in the 25·5 cm (10 in.) edges 4 cm (1½ in.) and stitch. This will leave enough fabric for an overlap of 4 cm (1½ in.) at the back of the bodice. Place the bodice on the child, overlapping and pinning the back edges. Mark the positions of the underarms, then take the bodice off the child and cut out two shallow semi-circles at the marked underarm positions. Turn in the upper edges 1·3 cm (½ in.) and stitch, clipping the underarm curves.

For each shoulder strap cut a 10 cm × 30·5 cm (4 in. × 12 in.) strip of fabric, fold along the length and sew the long edges together. Turn the straps right side out and press.

30

Put the bodice on the child with the right side of the fabric inside and overlap and pin the back edges. Pin the shoulder straps to the top edges to make the bodice fit neatly under the arms.

Pin a dart in the fabric at each side of the bodice to make it fit to the waist as shown in diagram 1. It may be necessary at this stage to cut the lower edge of the bodice to waist length if it is too long, but it should be left 1·3 cm ($\frac{1}{2}$ in.) longer than the child's waistline. Stitch the darts as pinned, then stitch the shoulder straps to the upper edge of the bodice at the front and back.

For each sleeve cut a 20·5 cm × 51 cm (8 × 20 in.) strip of fabric. Hem one long edge of each sleeve piece to form a casing for the elastic. Thread elastic through to fit the child's upper arms then sew the elastic in place at each end of the casing. Join the 20·5 cm (8 in.) edges of each sleeve piece.

Turn in the remaining raw edge of each sleeve and run a gathering thread through it. Slip stitch this edge to the shoulder strap and underarm curve as shown in diagram 2, pulling up the sleeve gathers to fit, and keeping most of the gathers at the top of the shoulder straps.

For the skirt cut a strip of fabric 1.9 m (2 yd) long (join shorter lengths if necessary) by 61 cm (24 in.) wide. Note that for a smaller child the width of this strip should be about two-thirds of the total skirt length from waist to floor level.

Join the short edges of the skirt strip, taking 4 cm (1$\frac{1}{2}$ in.) seam and leaving 15 cm (6 in.) open at the top of the seam for the back opening. Press the seam to one side.

For the skirt frill cut 35·5 cm (14 in.) wide strips (or one-third of the total skirt length measurement) about 2·8 m (3 yd) or more in length, according to the amount of fabric available. Join up the frill strips, then gather one long raw edge to fit the lower edge of the skirt and sew it in place.

Gather the upper edge of the skirt to fit the lower edge of the bodice and sew it in place. Turn up and stitch the hem edge of the frill. Sew braid or trimming and a ribbon bow to the bodice and skirt as shown in the illustration. Sew hooks and eyes or snap fasteners to the back bodice overlap.

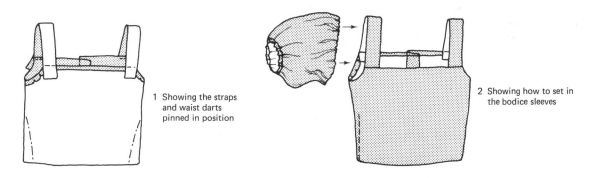

1 Showing the straps and waist darts pinned in position

2 Showing how to set in the bodice sleeves

For the wings cut a 1·9 m (2 yd) length of 92 cm (36 in.) wide transparent fabric. Fold it in half along the length, then in half again. Repeat this several times, then cut a scalloped shape through all thicknesses at one end so that when the strip is opened up again it is evenly scalloped along one edge. Attach the centre of the other long edge to the centre back neck edge of the dress bodice with a few stitches.

Make wrist bands to fit the child's wrists from strips of braid, fastening them with strips of *Velcro*. Attach the ends of the wings to the wristbands together with lengths of ribbon to hang down as illustrated.

To make the hat
For the hat, draw, then cut out a 35·5 cm (14 in.) radius quarter circle from the square of interlining. Spread a little glue all round the edges of the shape then place it on the wrong side of a piece of the left over dress fabric. Cut out the fabric along the edges of the hat shape. Overlap and glue the straight edges of the shape about 0·6 cm ($\frac{1}{4}$ in.) to form a cone shape, snipping about 2·5 cm (1 in.) off the top point in order to be able to do this.

Sew braid around the lower edge of the hat, then sew the remaining piece of transparent fabric and a length of ribbon to the top point.

Sew each end of a length of elastic to the inside of the lower edge of the hat to hold it firmly on the child's head.

Underskirt

To make the dress skirt stand out well an underskirt can be made from an old cotton sheet. Make it in the same way as the dress skirt, putting a little more fabric in to the frill if possible. Gather the waist edge on to a length of tape, leaving enough tape at each end for tying it around the waist.

Magic wand

Materials
A 51 cm (20 in.) length of thin wooden dowelling.
A star-shaped Christmas decoration.
Silver sticky tape.
Contact adhesive.

To make
Cover the dowelling by winding sticky tape around it, then glue the star to one end. Tie a bow of ribbon left over from making the dress to the wand.

Hot cross buns! Hot cross buns!
One a penny, two a penny,
Hot cross buns!

❧ *Hot Cross Buns* ❧

Instructions are given here for making all the items of clothing but ordinary pants, a shirt or sweater, and socks could be used as a basis. If ordinary pants are used the legs should be made to fit close to the child's legs by running a strong tacking thread parallel to the outside leg seam. The pants legs should then be turned up on the inside to make them just reach to the calf of the leg. A pair of old pants could also be altered permanently by cutting off the excess leg length. The hot cross buns are easy to make from felt and old nylon tights or stockings.

Striped socks

These are made from a piece of stretchy striped towelling. For one sock cut a 30·5 cm (12 in.) wide piece of towelling long enough to reach from the child's toe to well above the knee. The stripes should go around the leg. Pin the strip around the child's leg and foot with the right side of the fabric inside as shown in diagram 1, stretching the towelling to fit neatly as it is pinned on. This stretching process will shorten the sock so that it will reach just to the knee. Pull off the sock and stitch the seam as it is pinned. Trim off the excess fabric close to the seam. Hem the upper edge and thread through a length of elastic to fit the leg. Turn right side out and make another sock in the same way.

Buckled shoes

Black gym shoes are used with a metal buckle sewn to the front of each one. The tongues are made from felt stiffened by gluing it to thin card. Sew the centre bar of each buckle to each shoe. Cut the felt tongues to the correct width for threading through the buckles, making them wider at the top as shown in diagram 2. Thread

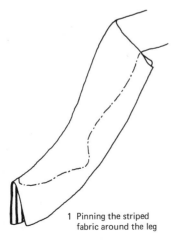

1 Pinning the striped fabric around the leg

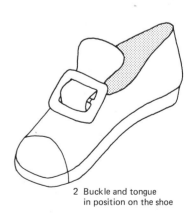

2 Buckle and tongue in position on the shoe

the tongues through the buckles, then put a dab of glue at the back of the buckles to hold the tongues in place.

Shirt and hat

Materials required for height 142 cm (4 ft 8 in.)
1·9 m (2 yd) of 92 cm (36 in.) wide white fabric, or cuttings from an old sheet.
46 cm ($\frac{1}{2}$ yd) of narrow elastic.
23 cm ($\frac{1}{4}$ yd) of 82 cm (32 in.) wide stiff white interlining.

To make the shirt
Use the tunic pattern given on page 10, shortening the sleeve edges to the lines marked B and shortening the lower edge to the line marked A. Cut the shirt from white fabric, then cut out the rounded neck edge about 1·3 cm ($\frac{1}{2}$ in.) lower than given on the tunic pattern.

Join the underarm and side seams and clip the underarm curves. Try the shirt on the child to see if larger turnings should be taken on these seams for a neater fit. Check also that the sleeve edges do not come too far down the arms, though they should come well off the shoulders for the dropped shoulder effect. Cut a little off the sleeve edges if necessary, then measure the distance from this edge to the child's knuckles. Cut a strip of fabric this length by 56 cm (22 in.) wide for each sleeve.

Fold each sleeve strip in half and join the edges which form the length of the sleeves. On each sleeve gather one 56 cm (22 in.) edge to fit the sleeve edge of the shirt and sew it in place. Gather the remaining 56 cm (22 in.) edges to fit the wrists loosely then bind these raw edges with bias strips of fabric.

Bind the neck edge with a bias strip of fabric and thread through elastic to fit the neck. Hem the lower edge of the shirt.

To make the hat

Cut a 15 cm (6 in.) wide strip of interlining long enough to go round the child's head plus 1.3 cm ($\frac{1}{2}$ in.). Overlap the 15 cm (6 in.) edges 1·3 cm ($\frac{1}{2}$ in.) and sew in place. To cover this tube shape cut a 20·5 cm (8 in.) wide strip of fabric the same length as the interlining strip. Join the 20·5 cm (8 in.) edges taking 0·6 cm ($\frac{1}{4}$ in.) seam. Turn right side out and place this tube over the interlining tube so that one raw edge and one edge of the interlining are even. The fabric tube will be 5 cm (2 in.) longer than the interlining tube at the other end as shown in diagram 3. Turn this raw edge of the fabric to the inside and stitch it to the edge of the interlining. Now turn up the remaining fabric which extends beyond the interlining tube to form a cuff as shown in diagram 4.

For the hat crown cut a 51 cm (20 in.) diameter circle of fabric. Turn in the edge 0·6 cm ($\frac{1}{4}$ in.) and run a gathering thread around it. Place the gathered circle right side out over the tube and pull up the gathers to fit. Sew the gathered edge to the outside of the tube about half way down, as shown in diagram 4.

Pants

Materials required for height 142 cm (4 ft 8 in.)
92 cm (1 yd) of 122 cm (48 in.) wide non-woven curtain fabric.
70 cm ($\frac{3}{4}$ yd) of 2·5 cm (1 in.) wide elastic.
Six buttons

To make
Use the pants pattern given on page 12, cutting the legs so that they will reach to just below knee length on the child. Make the pants following the instructions given with the pants pattern, then try them on the child with the wrong side outside. Pin a dart in each side of the pants to make them fit closely to the legs, taking care to leave them loose enough to be taken off. Sew the darts as pinned and then trim off the excess fabric. Hem the lower leg edges and turn the pants right side out. Sew three buttons to each side of the pants at the knee.

Neck scarf

Use a man's handkerchief.

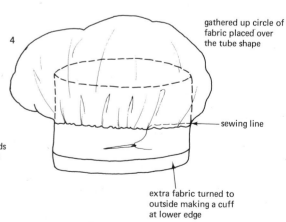

3

interlining tube inside fabric tube with upper edges even

seam

lower edge of interlining

fabric tube extends past interlining at lower edge

lower raw edge of fabric to be turned to inside and sewn to lower edge of interlining

4

gathered up circle of fabric placed over the tube shape

sewing line

extra fabric turned to outside making a cuff at lower edge

Apron

46 cm ($\frac{1}{2}$ yd) of 92 cm (36 in.) wide cotton fabric will make the apron. Cut a 46 cm × 56 cm (18 in. × 22 in.) piece off the fabric and use the remainder for the waistband. Pleat one 56 cm (22 in.) edge to measure 35·5 cm (14 in.) then hem the remaining raw edges. Sew the pleated edge to the waistband.

Tray of hot cross buns

Materials
Old nylon tights or stockings.
Brown and pale yellow felt.
A reddish brown pencil.
Cotton wool or kapok for stuffing the buns.
A cardboard grocery carton cut down to measure about 23 cm × 30·5 cm × 4 cm (9 in. × 12 in. × 1$\frac{1}{2}$ in.) deep, for the tray.
Piece of white fabric for the tray cloth.
4 cm (1$\frac{1}{2}$ in.) wide fawn coloured furnishing braid long enough to go round the sides of the tray.
A boot lace or length of cord for the neck strap.

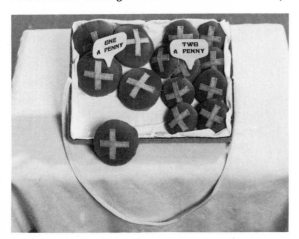

White card and two needles for the price tickets. Contact adhesive.

To make the tray
Glue the ends of the boot lace or cord to the sides of the tray and underneath, leaving the strap long enough so that the tray will be about waist height when worn. Glue the furnishing braid around the sides of the tray. Place the piece of fabric for the tray cloth in the tray and glue it down here and there to hold it in position.

To make the price tickets
Cut four price tickets from white card to the shape shown in the illustration. Glue them together in pairs, sandwiching the blunt end of a needle between each pair. Mark the words on each ticket.

To make the buns
For the 'one a penny' buns, cut a 13 cm (5 in.) diameter circle of nylon stocking fabric and a 10 cm (4 in.) diameter circle of brown felt. Run a gathering thread round the edge of the nylon circle then place the felt circle inside the nylon circle and stuff it firmly, pulling the gathering thread up tight to stretch the nylon fabric. The bun should measure about 9 cm (3$\frac{1}{2}$ in.) across. Fasten off the gathering thread.

Moisten the reddish brown pencil and rub it on top of the bun then rub the colour into the fabric with the finger tips. For the pastry crosses cut strips of yellow felt roughly 1·3 cm ($\frac{1}{2}$ in.) wide by 5·5 cm (2$\frac{1}{4}$ in.) long. Colour the edges of these felt strips with brown pencil before gluing them to the top of the bun.

Make the 'two a penny' buns in the same way using a 9 cm (3$\frac{1}{2}$ in.) diameter circle of nylon fabric, a 7 cm (2$\frac{3}{4}$ in.) diameter circle of felt and 4·5 cm (1$\frac{3}{4}$ in.) long strips for the pastry crosses. Glue the buns to the tray if desired.

'But Grandmamma, what big teeth you've got',
cried Red Riding Hood, and the Wolf sprang out of bed
growling 'All the better to EAT you with, my dear!'

Little Red Riding Hood

This is a quickly made costume using items of ordinary clothing and only two specially made garments.

Smock

Materials required for height 142 cm (4 ft 8 in.)
2·5 m (2¾ yd) of 92 cm (36 in.) wide cotton fabric.
7·8 m (8½ yd) of lace edging for trimming the dress and the collar and cuffs of the blouse.
5 cm (2 in.) strip of *Velcro* or snap fasteners for the back fastening.

To make
For the yoke of the smock cut a strip of fabric 13 cm (5 in.) wide, long enough to go around the child's chest just beneath the arms plus 10 cm (4 in.). Join the long edges of the strip and across one end, then turn right side out and press. Turn in the remaining raw edges and slip stitch. Sew *Velcro* or snap fasteners to the back edges.

For each shoulder strap cut a 13 cm (5 in.) wide by 35·5 cm (14 in.) long strip of fabric, join the long edges, turn the straps right side out and press. For each shoulder strap frill cut an 8 cm (3 in.) by 51 cm (20 in.) strip of fabric. Hem one long edge and sew on lace edging, then gather the other long edge to measure 35·5 cm (14 in.). Stitch one long edge of each shoulder strap to each frill, as shown in diagram 1, so that the frill is tapered toward each end.

Put the yoke on the child and place a strap over each shoulder, pinning the raw edges of the straps inside the band. Adjust the length of the straps as necessary, then stitch the ends of the straps in the pinned positions as shown in diagram 2.

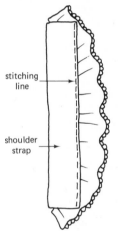

1 Stitching the shoulder strap to the frill

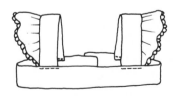

2 Showing positions of the straps on the yoke band

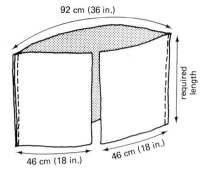

92 cm (36 in.)

required length

46 cm (18 in.)　　46 cm (18 in.)

3 Cutting one of the
skirt pieces open

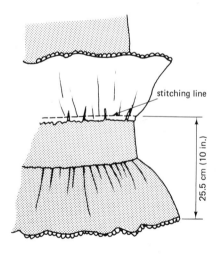

stitching line

25.5 cm (10 in.)

4 Showing how the second
skirt frill is sewn in place

For the skirt part of the smock cut two 92 cm (36 in.) wide pieces of fabric by the required length from the lower edge of the yoke to the child's knees. The frill at the hem adds the extra length later on.

Join the two pieces together at the short edges for the side seams then cut one piece in half from the hem to the top edge for the back opening as shown in diagram 3. Now join these edges once more from the hem to within 15 cm (6 in.) of the top edge taking a 2·5 cm (1 in.) seam. Press the seam to one side. The opening at the top is for the centre back opening of the smock. Gather the upper edge to fit the lower edge of the yoke band and sew in place.

For the hem frill cut three 15 cm (6 in.) by 92 cm (36 in.) strips of fabric and join them together at the short edges. Hem one long raw edge and stitch on lace edging. Gather the other long edge to fit the lower edge of the smock and sew it in place. Make another frill in the same way and stitch it to the smock 25·5 cm (10 in.) above the lower edge, as shown in diagram 4.

Blouse

Use an ordinary school blouse tacking lace edging to the edges of the collar and cuffs.

Hood

Materials required to fit any size
70 cm ($\frac{3}{4}$ yd) of 122 cm (48 in.) wide red curtain fabric.
1·4 m (1$\frac{1}{2}$ yd) of red bias binding.
A 30·5 cm (12 in.) length of elastic.
70 cm ($\frac{3}{4}$ yd) of lace trimming.
A white shoe lace or ribbon for the neck fastening.

To make

Cut a semi-circle from paper measuring 122 cm (48 in.) diameter, then cut this shape from fabric. Make a narrow hem all round the raw edges. For the casing for the elastic, stitch the bias binding to the wrong side of the fabric 25·5 cm (10 in.) from the curved edge. Thread the elastic through and stitch securely in place at each end. Sew lace trimming to the face edge of the hood. Cut the shoe lace or ribbon in half and sew each half in position for the ties at the ends of the elastic.

Shoes and socks

Ordinary shoes and socks can be worn, or slippers or ballet shoes.

Basket of goodies

Use a small toy shopping basket, filling it as desired and adding a small square of fabric fringed out at the edges for a napkin. The contents of the basket illustrated are listed here.

A small yellow plastic lid wrapped up in greaseproof paper for a pat of butter.

A small brown plastic container with melted candle wax inside and a circle of greaseproof paper tied on top for a pot of honey.

A wedge-shaped piece of cardboard wrapped up in tissue paper for a slice of cake.

Flowers

Use a few plastic 'wild' flowers such as primroses.

❧ *The Wolf* ❧

This is a suitable fancy dress for a boy or girl. Instructions are given for making the complete outfit as illustrated, but only the mask, nightcap and paws need to be made if the child already has a long nightdress or dressing gown to wear. For the shawl, a scarf or baby's shawl could be used.

Mask and paws

Materials required to fit any size
35 cm (⅜ yd) of 122 cm (48 in.) wide brown fur fabric.
23 cm (¼ yd) of 82 cm (32 in.) wide stiff white interlining for making the mask shape and for the teeth.
Scraps of felt, light brown, black, deep pink and orange.
Scrap of shiny black fabric such as taffeta for the nose, and cotton wool for stuffing.
70 cm (¾ yd) of 92 cm (36 in.) wide cotton fabric for the nightcap.
1·4 m (1½ yd) of lace edging for trimming the nightcap.
92 cm (1 yd) of narrow elastic.
A pair of spectacle frames or old sunglasses without lenses.
Contact adhesive.

To make the mask
The mask patterns are given here actual size. Trace them off the pages using thin paper, then cut out the pattern pieces. Join the edges of the face pieces marked A — B together with a bit of sticky tape to form the complete face pattern.

Cut out two face pieces from interlining, mark on the eye shapes and cut these out a little larger than the marked shapes. Join the two face pieces together along the upper edges taking the narrowest possible seam, then turn right side out.

Cut two face pieces from fur fabric adding 0·6 cm (¼ in.) extra on to the lower edges only, and taking care to reverse the pattern when

42

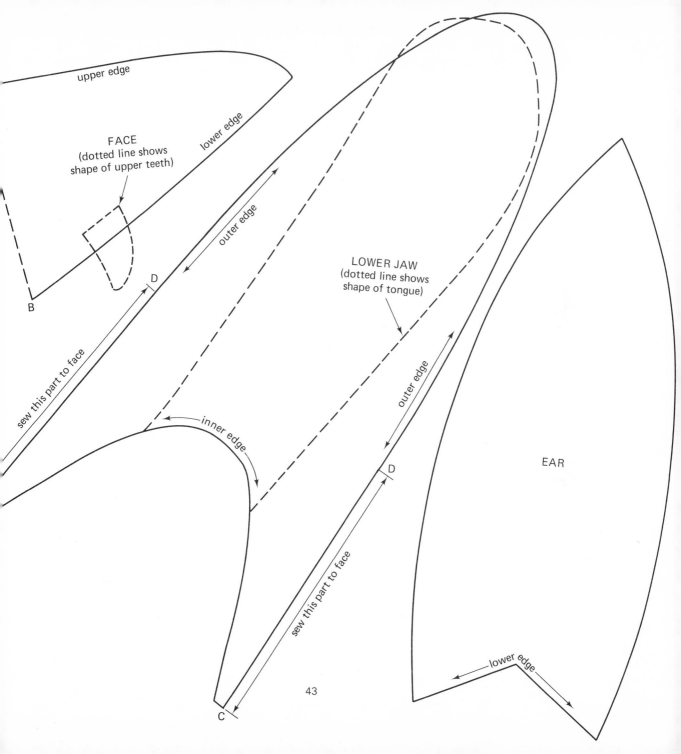

upper edge

FACE
(dotted line shows
shape of upper teeth)

lower edge

outer edge

D

B

LOWER JAW
(dotted line shows
shape of tongue)

outer edge

sew this part to face

inner edge

D

EAR

sew this part to face

C

lower edge

43

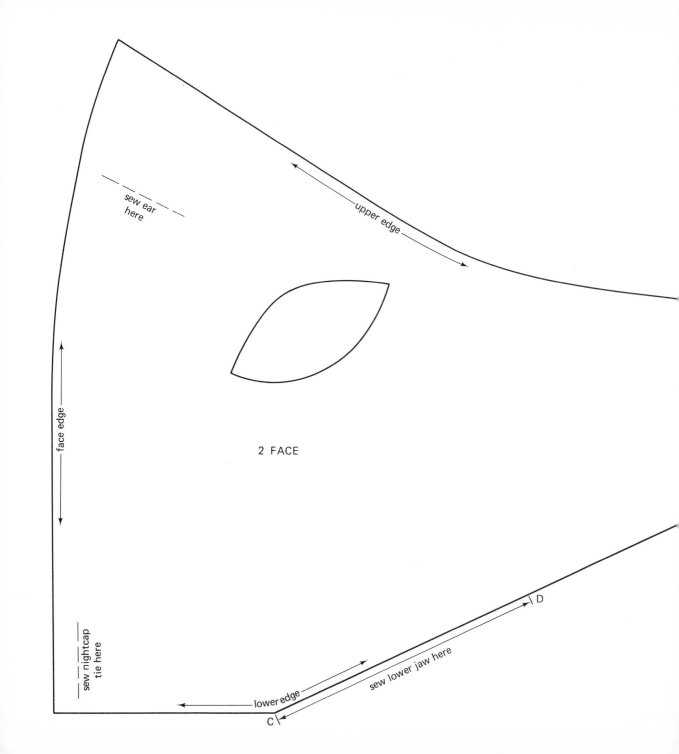

sew ear
here

upper edge

face edge

2 FACE

sew nightcap
tie here

lower edge

sew lower jaw here

C

D

cutting the second piece in order to make a pair. Mark on and cut out the eye shapes then join the pieces along the upper edges in the same way as the interlining pieces. Spread glue on the edges of the outside of the interlining mask and place the wrong side of the fur fabric mask on top of this. Turn the 0·6 cm ($\frac{1}{4}$ in.) extra at the lower edge of the fur fabric to the inside and glue in place. Cut two pieces of orange felt to fit behind the eye shapes, cutting out the eye holes slightly smaller than on the mask. Glue these pieces in place.

For the nose cut a 5 cm (2 in.) diameter circle of black fabric, run a gathering thread all round the edge, put a little cotton wool in the centre, pull up the gathers tightly and fasten off the thread. Sew the nose in place at the pointed end of the mask. Place the spectacle frames in position as illustrated then hold in place with a few stitches taken around the ear pieces and over the nose piece.

Cut two ear pattern pieces from interlining and glue them on to the wrong side of a piece of fur fabric. Cut out the fur fabric 0·6 cm ($\frac{1}{4}$ in.) larger all round the ears except for the lower edges. Fold over and glue down the 0·6 cm ($\frac{1}{4}$ in.) extra fur fabric on to the other side of the interlining. Cut two ear shapes from black felt and glue these on to the remaining uncovered part of the interlining for the insides of the ears. Fold each ear in half, bringing the lower edges together, oversew them together and then sew this edge of each ear to the mask at the position indicated on the face pattern.

Cut the lower jaw from two layers of interlining glued together to make it extra stiff. Keep the remains after cutting out for making the teeth. Glue the interlining lower jaw piece to the wrong side of a piece of fur fabric, then cut out the fur fabric 0·6 cm ($\frac{1}{4}$ in.) larger all round except for the inner edge. Fold over and glue

down the 0·6 cm ($\frac{1}{4}$ in.) extra fur fabric onto the other side of the interlining. Cut two upper teeth from interlining and glue them in place to the inside of the mask as shown on the face pattern. Cut a few more jagged shaped teeth and glue these upright round the lower jaw, even with the raw edge of the fur fabric.

Cut the lower jaw pattern piece from light brown felt and glue this to the remaining uncovered part of the interlining jaw. This will also help to keep the teeth in an upright position.

Cut the tongue from pink felt, using the dotted line shown on the lower jaw pattern as a guide. Glue the inner edge of the tongue to the inner edge of the lower jaw. Oversew the outer edge of the jaw to the lower edge of the mask at the position marked C – D on both pattern pieces.

To make the nightcap
Cut two 10 cm × 61 cm (4 in. × 24 in.) strips of fabric for the nightcap ties. Narrowly hem all the raw edges, then gather up and sew one short edge of each strip to either side of the mask at the position shown on the mask pattern.

For the nightcap cut two 28 cm × 61 cm (11 in. × 24 in.) strips of fabric, join the short edges, then turn in one long edge 6·5 cm (2$\frac{1}{2}$ in.) and press. Sew lace edging to the folded edge. Stitch the turned raw edge in place then work another line of stitching on the doubled fabric 1·3 cm ($\frac{1}{2}$ in.) from the first line to form a casing for the elastic. Thread through a 51 cm (20 in.) length of elastic and join the ends securely. Turn in the remaining long raw edge and run round a gathering thread. Pull up the gathers as tightly as possible and fasten off the thread.

Place the nightcap over the face edge of the mask and sew in place through the elastic, leaving about 20·5 cm (8 in.) of the nightcap free at the back, as shown in diagram 1, so that the mask can be put on the head.

To make the paws
For each paw cut two 11·5 cm × 25·5 cm (4½ in. × 10 in.) pieces of fur fabric. Join them in pairs round the edges leaving one 11·5 cm (4½ in.) edge open in each pair and rounding off the remaining corners. Trim the seams and corners and turn the paws right side out. Make two loops from the remainder of the elastic and wear these on the wrists on top of the paws to hold them in position.

Nightgown

Materials required for height 142 cm (4 ft 8 in.)
3·5 m (3¾ yd) of 92 cm (36 in.) wide fabric.
1·9 m (2 yd) of lace edging.
70 cm (¾ yd) of narrow elastic.
A few buttons.

To make
Use the tunic pattern given on page 10 altering it as follows: cut the sleeves to the line marked B, then cut the sleeve pattern separately, lengthening it so that it will reach to the child's wrists plus 10 cm (4 in.). Lengthen the lower edge of the tunic pattern to reach to the floor. Cut the curved neck edge about 2·5 cm (1 in.) lower than shown on the tunic pattern.

Cut the tunic and sleeves from fabric, then sew the upper edges of the sleeves to the sleeve edges of the tunic. Turn in the wrist edges of the sleeves 5 cm (2 in.) and make a casing for the elastic in the same way as for the nightcap. Stitch lace edging to the folded edge then thread a 15 cm (6 in.) length of elastic through each

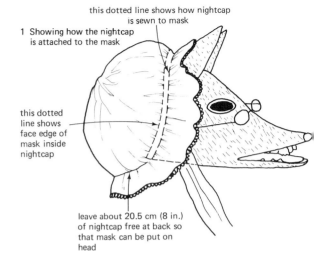

1 Showing how the nightcap is attached to the mask

this dotted line shows how nightcap is sewn to mask

this dotted line shows face edge of mask inside nightcap

leave about 20.5 cm (8 in.) of nightcap free at back so that mask can be put on head

wrist casing, sewing it securely in place at each end of the casing.

Join the entire side and sleeve seams of the nightgown, then clip the underarm curves. Hem the lower edge. Trim the centre front of the nightgown at the neck edge with a frill of lace and a few buttons, then bind the neck edge with a bias strip of fabric. Thread a 30·5 cm (12 in.) length of elastic through the binding and sew the ends together securely.

Shawl

Use a piece of blanket or sheeting about 76 cm (30 in.) square, hemming or fringing out the edges.

Feet

Brown socks to match the fur fabric, or slippers, can be worn.

The Queen of Hearts she made some tarts, all on a summer's day;
The Knave of Hearts he stole the tarts, and took them clean away.

❧ *The Queen of Hearts* ❧

The Queen wears an outfit in playing card colours of royal blue, red, yellow, white and black. A red T-shirt is used as a basis for the top of the costume; black, white and blue are also suitable colours. The heart-shaped tarts are made of yellow felt, red cellophane and foil sweet wrappings.

Skirt, top, collar and crown

Materials required for height 142 cm (4 ft 8 in.)
A red, white, black or blue T-shirt, either sleeve-less or with short sleeves.
1·9 m (2 yd) of 122 cm (48 in.) wide royal blue curtain fabric.
92 cm (1 yd) of 122 cm (48 in.) wide yellow curtain fabric.
46 cm (½ yd) of 92 cm (36 in.) wide white curtain net for the collar frill and the chin veil on the crown.
5·5 m (6 yd) of black bias binding.
2·8 m (3 yd) of yellow bias binding.
92 cm (1 yd) of red bias binding.
A length of 2·5 cm (1 in.) wide black petersham ribbon the child's waist measurement plus 8 cm (3 in.), for the skirt waistband.
15 cm (6 in.) strip of *Velcro* for skirt and back collar fastenings, or hooks and eyes instead.
Two strips of white fleecy fabric or felt measuring 6·5 cm × 61 cm (2½ in. × 24 in.).
Piece of red felt for the heart shapes, measuring 18 cm × 61 cm (7 in. × 24 in.).
46 cm (½ yd) of 82 cm (32 in.) wide stiff interlining for hat, collar and bodice front.
Contact adhesive.

To make the skirt
Cut a 1·9 m (2 yd) long strip of royal blue fabric making the width the measurement from the child's waist to floor level as shown in diagram 1. The remaining piece of fabric is for the sleeves. Cut out the four sleeve pieces as shown in diagram 1.

48

From the yellow fabric cut the strip which will be sewn to the centre front of the skirt. This should measure 9 cm (3½ in.) in width at the waist edge, broadening out to 35·5 cm (14 in.) at the hem, and the same length exactly as for the skirt length. Glue the raw edges of this piece to the skirt then sew on black bias binding to cover the long raw edges of the yellow strip.

From red felt cut out the largest heart shape to the size shown in diagram 2 then cut out four more hearts making each one about 0·6 cm (¼ in.) smaller all round than the one before. Glue or sew the hearts in place on the yellow skirt strip as illustrated.

Join the short edges of the skirt for the centre back seam from the hem edge to within 15 cm (6 in.) of the waist edge, taking a 2·5 cm (1 in.) seam. Press the seam to one side. The opening at the top forms the skirt opening. Gather the waist edge of the skirt to fit the child's waist, sew it to the length of ribbon then sew *Velcro* or hooks and eyes at the waistband overlap. Hem the lower edge of the skirt.

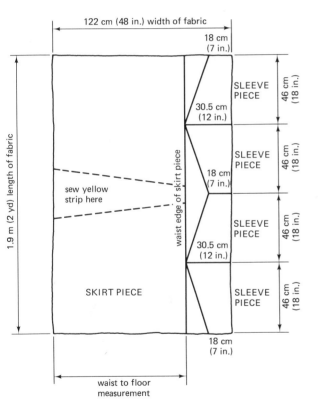

1 Cutting the blue fabric
   for the skirt and sleeves

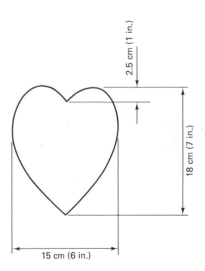

2 Largest heart shape
   on skirt

To make the dress top

Join the sleeve pieces in pairs along the 46 cm (18 in.) edges. These form the overarm seams. Join the tapered edges for the underarm seams. Turn in the narrow ends which are the armhole edges of the sleeves, and tack or stitch these to the armholes of the T-shirt. If the T-shirt has short sleeves these will be inside the blue fabric sleeves. Try the dress top on the child to see if the wrist edges of the sleeves need to be shortened and cut off any excess.

Turn the wrist edges of the sleeves 0·6 cm ($\frac{1}{4}$ in.) to the outside and press.

Bind the long edges of the strips of white fleecy fabric or felt with yellow bias binding, then sew each one round the wrist edge of each sleeve to cover the raw edges.

Cut sixteen red felt hearts to the size shown in diagram 3 and glue eight to each white fleecy strip as illustrated.

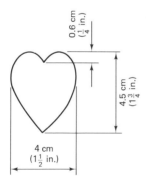

0·6 cm ($\frac{1}{4}$ in.)

4·5 cm ($1\frac{3}{4}$ in.)

4 cm ($1\frac{1}{2}$ in.)

3 Small heart shape

From the yellow fabric cut the strip which will be sewn to the centre front of the T-shirt. This should measure 15 cm (6 in.) at the top edge tapering to 9 cm ($3\frac{1}{2}$ in.) at the lower edge by 35·5 cm (14 in.) in length. Cut a piece of interlining the same size and glue it to the wrong side of the yellow strip. Bind the long raw edges of the strip with black bias binding and tack or stitch it round the edges to the centre front of the T-shirt.

To make the collar

Cut a 40·5 cm (16 in.) diameter circle of interlining with a 13 cm (5 in.) diameter hole cut out of the centre for the neck edge. Cut away one quarter of the circle and discard it. Glue the interlining collar shape on to the wrong side of a piece of yellow fabric then cut out the fabric even with the interlining. Cover the other side of the interlining in the same way.

Sew a strip of black bias binding round the collar about 4 cm ($1\frac{1}{2}$ in.) from the outer edge, then bind the outer edge and the short straight edges with black bias.

For the collar frill cut a 20·5 × 86·5 cm (8 in. × 34 in.) strip of white net fabric, fold in half widthways and gather up the long edges to fit the neck edge of the collar. Stitch the gathered edge of the frill in place. Bind the neck edge of the collar with red bias, then sew an 8 cm (3 in.) strip of *Velcro* or hooks and eyes to the short straight edges for the back collar fastening.

To make the crown

Cut a 13 cm (5 in.) wide strip of interlining to fit around the child's head plus 0·6 cm ($\frac{1}{4}$ in.) for the overlap. Cover both sides of the interlining with yellow fabric in the same way as for the collar. Fold the strip into four along the length, then along one side cut out a curve through all thicknesses using the edge of a saucer as a guide. This will give the crown four points when the strip is opened up. Bind the upper curved edges with black bias and the lower edge with red bias. Overlap the short edges 0·6 cm ($\frac{1}{4}$ in.)

and glue or stitch in place. Cut out four red felt hearts to the size shown in diagram 3 and glue them to the crown as illustrated.

For the chin veil, cut an 18 cm × 40·5 cm (7 in. × 16 in.) strip of white net fabric and hem the edges. Gather up the short edges and sew one to each side of the crown to pass under the chin.

Hip pad

To make the skirt stand out around the hips make a hip pad from a nylon stocking stuffed into a sausage shape about 56 cm (22 in.) in length. Gather each end and sew on a length of tape so that the pad can be tied on just below the child's waist.

Plate of tarts

Materials
A piece of yellow or fawn felt for the pastry.
Red cellophane and foil sweet wrappings for the jam.
A paper plate or small baking tray.
Brown and red felt-tipped pens.
Contact adhesive.

To make
For one tart cut out two heart shapes from felt to the sizes shown in diagram 4. Cut the centre

out of one heart shape and discard it, leaving about 0·6 cm ($\frac{1}{4}$ in.) round the edges as shown by the dotted line on the diagram.

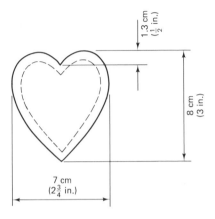

4 Heart shape for the tarts

Cut heart shapes from foil and cellophane making them slightly smaller all round. Glue the foil to the felt heart, the cellophane to the foil and finally glue the felt heart with the cut out centre on top.

Colour the outer edges of the felt with brown pen and the inner edges with red. Make as many tarts as desired and glue them to the plate or tray.

The Knave wears a costume to match the Queen's. A long sleeved T-shirt, shirt or sweater, and tights are used as a basis for the outfit. These can be in any of the playing card colours of royal blue, red, yellow, white or black.

Sweater and tights

Any of the colours listed above are suitable.

Shoes

Use black gym shoes. Cut two heart shapes from red felt about the size of the tarts given in diagram 4 in the Queen of Hearts instructions. Glue or pin the hearts to the fronts of the shoes as illustrated.

Tunic, collar, cuffs and crown

Materials required for height 142 cm (4 ft 8 in.)
1·4 m (1½ yd) of 122 cm (48 in.) wide royal blue curtain fabric.
92 cm (1 yd) of 122 cm (48 in.) wide yellow curtain fabric.
92 cm (1 yd) of ready frilled lace edging for the collar and cuff frills.
4·4 m (4¾ yd) of black bias binding.
1·2 m (1¼ yd) of broad black ric-rac braid for trimming the collar.
1·9 m (2 yd) of yellow bias binding.
92 cm (1 yd) of red bias binding.
13 cm (5 in.) strip of *Velcro* for back collar fastening or hooks and eyes instead.

52

Two strips of white fleecy fabric or felt measuring 6·5 cm × 46 cm (2½ in. × 18 in.).
Piece of red felt for the heart shapes measuring 25·5 cm × 46 cm (10 in. × 18 in.).
70 cm (¾ yd) of 82 cm (32 in.) wide stiff interlining for collar, cuffs and crown.
Contact adhesive.

To make the tunic
Use the tunic pattern given on page 10, shortening the sleeve edges to the lines marked B. Place the pattern against the child to check that the hem edge comes slightly lower than the tops of the legs and shorten or lengthen the pattern as necessary.

Cut the tunic from royal blue fabric, then cut out the V-neckline on the front of the tunic only. For the yellow panel down the front of the tunic cut a strip of yellow fabric measuring 15 cm (6 in.) across at the neck edge and broadening out to 30·5 cm (12 in.) at the hem edge of the tunic. Glue the raw edges of this piece to the centre front of the tunic, then sew on black bias binding to cover the long raw edges of the yellow strip. Bind the neck edge with black bias binding.

From red felt cut out the largest heart shape as given in diagram 2 in the Queen of Hearts instructions, then cut out another heart about 0·6 cm (¼ in.) smaller all round. Glue or sew the hearts to the yellow strip as illustrated.

Join the side and underarm seams of the tunic and clip the underarm curves. Try the tunic on the child to see if larger turnings need to be taken on these seams to make the tunic fit neatly. Hem the sleeve and lower edges.

To make the collar
Cut a 43 cm (17 in.) square of stiff interlining. Cut away one quarter of this square and discard it. Draw and cut out a 15 cm (6 in.) diameter

circle at the centre of the square as shown in diagram 1. This forms the collar shape. Try the collar shape on the child, bringing the centre back edges together, then trim a little off the outer edges if the collar looks too large for the child.

Spread glue on the edges of one side of the collar and place it on a piece of the yellow fabric, then cut out the fabric even with the collar shape. Repeat this on the other side of the interlining. Bind the neck edge of the collar with red bias binding and the remaining raw edges with black bias binding. Sew on the ric-rac braid as illustrated. Glue or sew on a heart shape cut from red felt, making it about 0·6 cm (¼ in.) smaller all round than the smallest heart on the tunic. Sew frilled edging to the neck edge of the collar and then sew *Velcro* or hooks and eyes to the centre back edges.

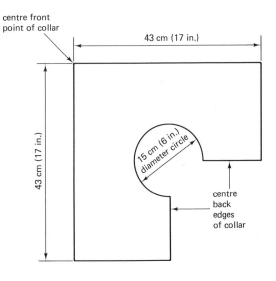

1 The collar shape

To make the cuffs and crown

Make a paper pattern for these by drawing and cutting out a 71 cm (28 in.) diameter semi-circle. Draw another two semi-circles within the first, making one 56 cm (22 in.) diameter and one 25.5 cm (10 in.) diameter as shown in diagram 2. Cut out the 25·5 cm (10 in.) diameter semi-circle and discard it. Cut out the 56 cm (22 in.) diameter semi-circle and cut it in half on the dotted line indicated in the diagram; use only one of these pieces for the cuff pattern.

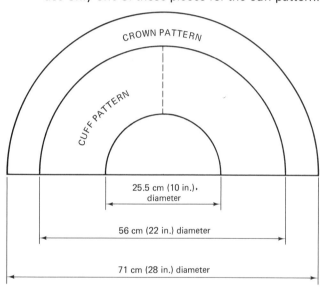

25.5 cm (10 in.) diameter

56 cm (22 in.) diameter

71 cm (28 in.) diameter

2 The crown and cuff pattern shapes

The remaining narrow piece is the crown pattern. Place it on the child's head, overlapping and cutting the short edges to make it fit, leaving 0·6 cm ($\frac{1}{4}$ in.) extra for an overlap.

Cut two cuff pieces from interlining and cover both sides of each piece with royal blue fabric in the same way as for the collar. Overlap the straight edges of each cuff 0·6 cm ($\frac{1}{4}$ in.) and glue, and try the cuffs on the child to see that they will slide over the hands easily. If the narrow end is too tight trim a little off it. If the cuffs are too long for the child, trim the other ends to size. Sew frilled edging to the narrow wrist edges of the cuffs.

Bind one long edge of each strip of white fabric or felt with yellow bias binding, stretching the binding as it is sewn on to draw up the edge of the white fabric and make it shorter. Join the short edges of each white strip. Tack the remaining raw edges of the white strips to the wide edges of the cuffs with the raw edges even. Bind these edges with yellow bias binding.

For each cuff cut out six small red felt heart shapes as given in diagram 3 in the Queen of Hearts' instructions. Glue them to the white fabric at even intervals as shown in the illustration.

Cut the crown shape from interlining then cover both sides with yellow fabric in the same way as given for the collar. Overlap the short edges of the crown 0·6 cm ($\frac{1}{4}$ in.) and glue. Bind the upper edge with black bias binding and the lower edge with red. Cut out four red felt heart shapes and glue them to the crown at intervals as illustrated.

Plate of tarts

Make in the same way as given for the Queen of Hearts.

The Frog Prince and the Princess

*. . . and the frog hopped into the deep pool
and brought out the Princess' golden ball*

❧ *The Frog Prince* ☙

The frog is in fact a little floppy 'bean' bag made from velvet and filled with either rice or lentils.

Materials
Two 20·5 cm (8 in.) squares of green velvet or felt, if possible having one square a shade lighter than the other.
140 g (5 oz.) of rice or lentils.
Two 1·3 cm ($\frac{1}{2}$ in.) diameter black or brown beads for eyes.
Scrap of orange felt.
Black permanent marker pen.
Contact adhesive.

To make
The frog patterns are given here actual size. Trace them off the page using thin paper then cut out the paper patterns. Place the two squares of velvet or felt right sides together and pin the body pattern on to this double thickness. Machine stitch all round the paper shape, exactly at the edges, leaving a gap in the seam as indicated on the pattern. Remove the paper pattern then cut out the frog about 0·3 cm ($\frac{1}{8}$ in.) from the line of stitching. Turn right side out.

Fill the frog with the rice or lentils using a little funnel shape made from paper to do this more easily. Turn in the remaining raw edges and slip stitch the gap. Mark the darker side of the frog with spots and blotches as illustrated using black pen.

Cut 0·3 cm ($\frac{1}{8}$ in.) wide strips of orange felt and glue around each bead making the hole in the bead the centre of the eye as shown in diagram 1. Cut a 5 cm (2 in.) square of the darker green velvet or felt from the pieces left over after cutting out the frog. Spread glue on the wrong side of the square and fold it in half with the glued sides together. From this piece, cut out two eyelids placing the eyelid pattern against the fold in the fabric as shown on the pattern. Glue an eyelid over each eye then glue the eyes in place as shown on the pattern.

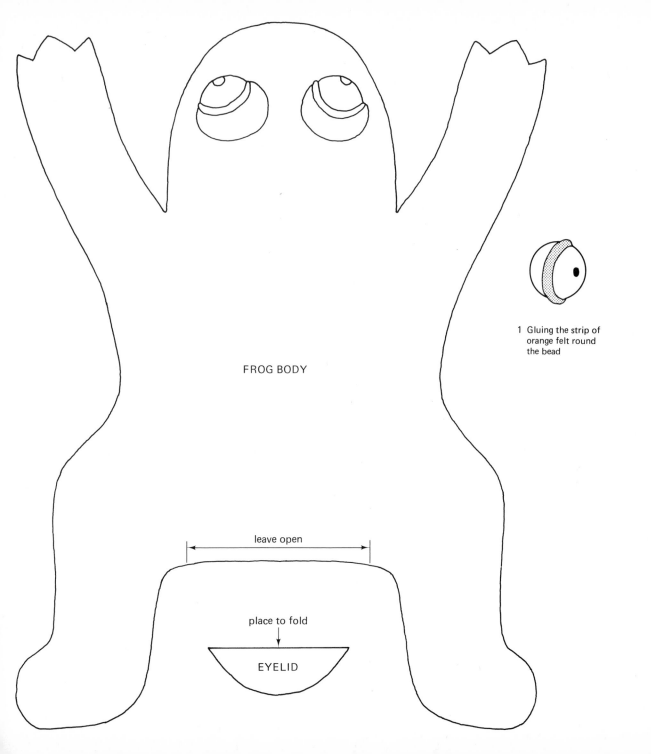

FROG BODY

1 Gluing the strip of
orange felt round
the bead

leave open

place to fold

EYELID

✻✿ *The Princess* ✿✻

The princess outfit is very quick and easy to make.

The princess's dress and head band

Materials required for height 142 cm (4 ft 8 in.)
2·8 cm (3 yd) of 122 cm (48 in.) wide brocade curtain fabric.
5·5 m (6 yd) of braid for edging the dress and the undersleeves and for the head band.
23 cm ($\frac{1}{4}$ yd) of 122 cm (48 in.) wide curtain velvet for the undersleeves and neck trimming.
46 cm ($\frac{1}{2}$ yd) of narrow elastic.
2·8 m (3 yd) of thick silky dressing gown cord for the girdle.
A chiffon scarf or piece of thin fabric for the veil.

To make
Use the tunic pattern given on page 10 as a basis for cutting out the dress as shown in diagram 2. Cut the sleeve edges to the full width of the fabric taking the underarm sleeve edges almost to the full length of the fabric. Cut the lower edge to the required length to make the dress floor level on the child. Cut out the V-neckline on the front and the back of the dress.

Join the entire side and underarm sleeve seams of the dress and clip the underarm curves. Try the dress on the child to see if larger underarm seams need to be taken; this will probably be necessary to give a neater armhole fit.

Now join the sleeve edges from the pointed end to within 38 cm (15 in.) of the upper folded edge. Turn the dress right side out then turn in and hem the remaining raw edges of the sleeves.

Cut the front V-neckline a little lower than the back, then turn in the neck edge 0·6 cm ($\frac{1}{4}$ in.) and stitch, clipping the edge if necessary to make it turn. Hem the lower edge of the dress.

Stitch braid trimming to the neck, sleeve and lower edges. Run a gathering thread along the top folded edge of each sleeve from the braid trimming for 20·5 cm (8 in.) as shown in diagram 2, pull up the gathers tightly and fasten off the threads.

For each undersleeve cut a 23 cm × 40·5 cm (9 in. × 16 in.) strip of velvet. With the right side

inside pin the strips around the child's arms as shown in diagram 3, with the 40·5 cm (16 in.) length along the length of the arms. The fabric should come well down over the hands and the sleeves should be pinned loosely enough to be taken off and on. Take off the sleeves and sew the seams as pinned. Trim off the excess fabric at the seams and then hem the upper and lower edges. Trim the lower edges with braid and thread elastic through the upper edges to fit the child's arms.

For the velvet piece at the front neck edge of the dress, cut a triangle of velvet to fit, hem and trim the upper edge with braid, then sew the triangle in position on the inside of the dress.

For the head band cut a length of braid to go around the child's head plus a little extra for a seam. Sew the ends of the braid together then sew the scarf or fabric to the head band to hang down the back as illustrated.

For the girdle tie a knot in each end of the cord and tie it around the dress as illustrated.

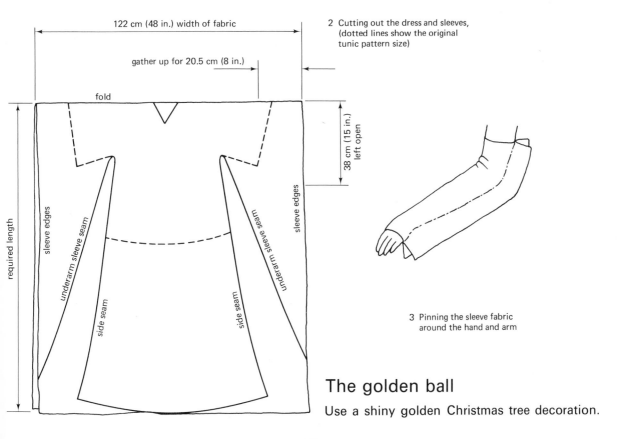

122 cm (48 in.) width of fabric

gather up for 20.5 cm (8 in.)

fold

required length

sleeve edges

underarm sleeve seam

side seam

side seam

underarm sleeve seam

sleeve edges

38 cm (15 in.) left open

2 Cutting out the dress and sleeves, (dotted lines show the original tunic pattern size)

3 Pinning the sleeve fabric around the hand and arm

The golden ball

Use a shiny golden Christmas tree decoration.

Wee Willie Winkie runs through the town,
Upstairs and downstairs in his night-gown,
Rapping at the window, crying through the lock,
Are the children all in bed, for now it's eight o'clock?

✤ *Wee Willie Winkie* ✤

A simple costume made from striped fabric which looks best on a small child. The lantern is easy to make using a lampshade frame as a basis. A tube of card makes the candle with a twist of cellophane for the flame.

Nightshirt and nightcap

Materials required for height 122 cm (4 ft)
2·8 m (3 yd) of 92 cm (36 in.) wide striped fabric.
46 cm ($\frac{1}{2}$ yd) of 92 cm (36 in.) wide plain fabric for the frills.
46 cm ($\frac{1}{2}$ yd) of narrow elastic.
A few buttons.
Cotton wool for stuffing the nightcap bobble.

To make the nightshirt
Use the tunic pattern given on page 10 altering it as follows: cut the sleeves to the line marked B, then cut the sleeve pattern separately lengthening it so that it will reach to the child's wrists plus 2·5 cm (1 in.). Lengthen the lower edge of the tunic pattern to reach to mid-calf length on the child. Cut the curved neck edge about 1·3 cm ($\frac{1}{2}$ in.) lower than given on the tunic pattern. Cut the hem edge in a curve at the side seams to make curved side slits.

Cut the nightshirt and sleeves from fabric, then join the top edges of the sleeves to the sleeve edges of the nightshirt. From the plain fabric cut two 8 cm (3 in.) wide strips the length of the wrist edges on the nightshirt sleeves. Sew one long edge of each strip to each wrist edge, then stitch the seam down flat to the sleeve fabric to form a casing for the elastic.

Hem the remaining long edges of the plain fabric.

Thread a length of elastic through each casing to fit the wrists, securing the elastic at each end of the casing with a few stitches. Join the side and underarm seams and clip the underarm curves. Hem the lower edge of the nightshirt.

For the neck frill cut two 8 cm × 92 cm (3 in. × 36 in.) strips of plain fabric. Join the strips at the short edges. Hem one of the long raw edges and gather the other long raw edge to measure about 102 cm (40 in.). Pin the frill around the neck edge of the nightshirt with the raw edges of the frill and nightshirt even, then pin the excess frill in a double row down the centre front as illustrated. Sew the frill in place, then bind the raw neck edges with a bias strip of fabric to form a casing for the elastic. Thread through elastic to fit the child's neck then sew buttons down the centre of the double frill.

To make the nightcap
Cut a 35·5 cm (14 in.) wide strip of striped fabric long enough to go around the child's head plus 2·5 cm (1 in.). Cut an 8 cm (3 in.) wide strip of plain fabric the same length and sew one long edge of this to one long edge of the striped fabric. Join the 35·5 cm (14 in.) edges then turn the plain fabric band to the inside and stitch down the raw edge. On the wrong side of the cap gather the remaining raw edge up tightly and fasten off the gathering thread. Turn right side out.

For the bobble cut a 13 cm (5 in.) diameter circle of plain fabric, run a gathering thread round the edge, stuff the centre with cotton wool and pull up the gathers and fasten off. Sew the bobble to nightcap.

The lantern

Materials

A small lampshade frame; the one illustrated measures 13 cm (5 in.) diameter at the widest end, 9 cm (3½ in.) diameter at the narrow end and 15 cm (6 in.) in height. It has four struts and a flat ring fitting.

A cardboard sweet tube about 2·5 cm (1 in.) in diameter, or thin card.

Thin card for the top of the lantern.

Red and yellow cellophane sweet wrappings and a piece of string for the candle flame.

3·7 cm (4 yd) of 1·3 cm (½ in.) wide lampshade braid in a dark colour.

Contact adhesive.

To make

Cut a circle of card to fit inside the lampshade frame at the narrowest end. This will be the base of the lantern. Glue the card in place. Glue strips of braid to the outside of the four metal struts, then glue on four more lengths between the struts making eight struts altogether. Glue a length of braid around the ring at the base and another length about half way up from the base.

For the candle use a cardboard sweet tube cut down to about 8 cm (3 in.) in height or make a similar tube from thin card. Cover the tube with white paper and glue a circle of card just inside one end for the top of the candle. Use a short length of string for the wick and on to this twist and glue a piece of red and yellow cellophane for the flame. Pierce the card at the top of the candle and glue the wick in the hole. Dribble some contact adhesive down the side of the candle to resemble runs of wax, and allow to dry. Glue the candle to the base of the lamp and then glue a bit of braid round the bottom of the candle.

For the top of the lantern cut a 23 cm (9 in.) diameter circle of card. Cut away one quarter of the circle and discard it. Bring the straight edges together and hold them in place on the inside with a piece of sticky tape. Spread glue liberally on the top ring of the lantern and stick the cardboard top in position. Glue strips of braid over the top to match the struts, then glue braid round the edge of the cardboard and a braid ring on top for carrying the lantern.

Bedsocks and slippers

Use brightly coloured slippers and socks.

*Goldilocks ran towards the open window of the cottage
as fast as she could*

✥ Goldilocks ✥

Goldilocks wears a crinoline petticoat under her skirt. The petticoat stands out in the required shape by means of two hoops made from polyester boning, which is sold for stiffening and boning dress bodices, etc. As an alternative, a couple of very full underskirts made from an old sheet could be worn under the skirt.

Blouse

Use an ordinary school blouse, tacking lace edging to the edge of the collar.

Pantaloons

Materials required for height 142 cm (4 ft 8 in.)
1·9 m (2 yd) of 92 cm (36 in.) wide white cotton fabric or cuttings from an old sheet.
70 cm ($\frac{3}{4}$ yd) of 2·5 cm (1 in.) wide elastic.
1·4 m (1$\frac{1}{2}$ yd) of narrow white lace edging.

To make
Use the pants pattern given on page 12 cutting the legs long enough to reach the child's ankles. Make up the pants as in the instructions given with the pants pattern, then sew two rows of lace trimming to the lower edges.

Skirt and false sleeves

Materials required for height 142 cm (4 ft 8 in.)
1·9 m (2 yd) of 92 cm (36 in.) wide printed fabric.
Velcro or hooks and eyes for the waistband fastening.
92 cm (1 yd) of narrow elastic.

To make the skirt
Cut two 92 cm (36 in.) wide strips of fabric 66 cm (26 in.) long, or adjust this measurement to make the skirt a suitable length for the child, noting that when the crinoline is worn underneath the skirt the hemline will be higher.

Join the short edges of the strips leaving a 15 cm (6 in.) gap at the top of one seam for the side opening. Gather up the waist edge to fit the child's waist measurement. Cut an 8 cm (3 in.) wide strip of fabric for the skirt waistband and sew it to the gathered waist edge. Sew *Velcro* or hooks and eyes to the waistband at the overlap. Do not hem the lower edge of the skirt at this stage.

To make the false sleeves
Cut two 35·5 cm × 46 cm (14 in. × 18 in.) pieces of fabric, noting that there should now be a narrow strip of fabric left over for making the bow on the jacket. Join the 35·5 cm (14 in.) edges of each sleeve piece. Hem the remaining raw edges and thread elastic through each hem to fit the child's wrists at one end of the sleeves and the upper arms at the other end.

Crinoline petticoat

Materials required for height 142 cm (4 ft 8 in.)
Two strips of cotton fabric the same size as the skirt pieces.
3·2 m (3½ yd) of 1·3 cm (½ in.) wide polyester boning.

To make
Join the short edges of the strips of fabric leaving a gap at the top of one seam in the same way as for the skirt. Make two 2 cm (¾ in.) tucks all round the petticoat on the outside, one about 8 cm (3 in.) above the hem edge and the next 13 cm (5 in.) above the first, as shown in diagram 1. Now stitch the folded edge of each of these tucks flat down on to the skirt, thus forming casings through which the boning can be threaded. Leave a gap in the stitching so that the boning can be inserted. For the lower hoop, thread through a 1·7 m (66 in.) length of boning,

overlap the ends of the boning and oversew securely. Thread the remainder of the boning through the upper casing and sew the ends together as before. Space out the fullness of the fabric evenly all round the boning.

Gather the upper edge of the petticoat to fit the waist edge of the skirt and sew it inside the skirt waistband. Now try the skirt on the child and adjust the hem edges to the required lengths. Hem the lower edges.

Jacket

Materials required for height 142 cm (4 ft 8 in.)
92 cm (1 yd) of 92 cm (36 in.) wide non-woven fabric.
A hook and eye.

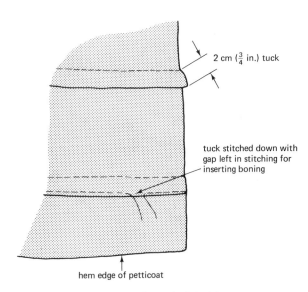

2 cm (¾ in.) tuck

tuck stitched down with gap left in stitching for inserting boning

hem edge of petticoat

1 Showing first tuck stitched down and second tuck before stitching down

To make

Use the tunic pattern given on page 10, shortening the sleeve edges by about 5 cm (2 in.) and making the length of the tunic the child's neck to waist measurement. Cut the tunic shape from fabric, then cut out the rounded neckline. To make the centre front opening on the jacket, cut the tunic open down the centre front from the hem edge to the neck edge.

Join the side and underarm seams and clip the underarm curves. Try the jacket on the child and check to see if larger turnings need to be taken on these seams to make the jacket fit neatly as shown in the illustration.

Take narrow hems on all the raw edges to neaten them, clipping the neck edge if necessary at intervals. Sew on the hook and eye at the front neck edges. Use the strip of printed fabric to make a bow and sew this to the neck edge at one side so that the bow will be in the centre when the jacket is fastened.

Bonnet

Materials required to fit all sizes

A strip of stiff white interlining measuring 13 cm × 40·5 cm (5 in. × 16 in.) for the brim shape.
58 cm ($\frac{5}{8}$ yd) of 92 cm (36 in.) wide white cotton fabric.
1·4 m (1$\frac{1}{2}$ yd) of narrow white lace edging.

To make

Cut two corners of the interlining strip into a rounded shape as shown in diagram 2. To cover the brim, cut two pieces of fabric the same as the brim making the fabric pieces 1·3 cm ($\frac{1}{2}$ in.) larger all round except for the back edges.

Join the fabric pieces leaving the back edges open. Trim the seam and turn right side out. Slip the interlining brim shape inside the fabric brim and tack the remaining raw edges together.

For the back of the bonnet cut a 40·5 cm (16 in.) diameter circle of fabric. Fold the circle in half and run a gathering thread round the curved edges through both thicknesses of fabric. Pull up the gathers to fit the back edge of the brim, then sew the gathered edge to the back edge. Gather up the straight edge of the back of the bonnet to measure 20·5 cm (8 in.).

For the back frill cut a 15 cm × 40·5 cm (6 in. × 16 in.) strip of fabric, fold it in half widthways and stitch across the short edges. Turn right side out and press. Gather up the remaining raw edges to measure 20·5 cm (8 in.) and sew to the 20·5 cm (8 in.) gathered edge of the bonnet. Sew lace edging all round the edges of the bonnet.

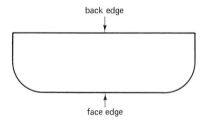

back edge

face edge

2 Rounding off two corners of the brim shape

Socks and shoes

Ballet shoes, slippers or ordinary shoes and socks can be worn.

❧ *Baby Bear* ❧

Baby bear wears an old-fashioned sailor suit which is easy to make using navy blue pyjamas as a basis. The pyjamas can be altered temporarily if desired and any plain colour is suitable. Items of the child's ordinary clothing could of course be worn instead with only the mask and paws being specially made. If a small child wears the Baby Bear costume then Father and Mother bear costumes could be made for taller children to complete the family.

Sailor suit

Materials required for any size
A pair of pyjamas to fit the child.
23 cm ($\frac{1}{4}$ yd) of 92 cm (36 in.) wide striped fabric in red, white or blue. The fabric used in the outfit illustrated has blue and red stripes, and the white stripes on the cuffs and knee bands are made by stitching on strips of white tape. Alternatively, plain coloured fabric can be used, making the contrasting stripes from coloured tape.
70 cm ($\frac{3}{4}$ yd) of narrow elastic.
4 snap fasteners.
92 cm (1 yd) of ribbon for the bow on the collar.
46 cm ($\frac{1}{2}$ yd) of 92 cm (36 in.) wide white fabric for the collar.
1·2 m (1$\frac{1}{4}$ yd) of ric-rac braid for trimming the collar.

To make the knickerbockers
Put the pyjama pants on the child and turn the pants legs up to the inside making the lower edges just below knee length. Pin the folded

edges of the pants legs in this position. If the alteration is to be permanent, cut off the excess leg length.

Gather up the lower edges of the pants legs to fit the legs. Sew or tack a band of striped fabric to the gathered edge of each leg making sure that the band is loose enough for the pants to be put on and off when the child has socks on.

To make the sailor top and collar
Run a length of elastic through the hem edge of the pyjama top to fit the child's hips and sew the elastic in place at each end. Sew a snap fastener to the hem edges at each end.

Sew or tack a striped band to the wrist edge of each sleeve to match the knickerbocker bands.

Draw out a paper pattern for the collar as given in diagram 1. Cut out two collar pieces from the white fabric, placing the edge marked 'fold' against a fold in the fabric. On one of the collar pieces stitch ric-rac braid 5 cm (2 in.) in from the three straight edges. Now join the

46 cm (18 in.)

fold

23 cm (9 in.)

19 cm (7½ in.)

1 The collar pattern

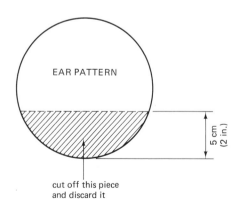

EAR PATTERN

5 cm (2 in.)

cut off this piece and discard it

2 Making the ear pattern

collar pieces all round the edges leaving a gap in the seam for turning right side out. Trim the seam and turn right side out. Press the collar, then slip stitch the opening.

Put the pyjama top on the child back to front then put on the collar. Mark the position where the points of the collar meet at the centre front. Cut a triangle of striped fabric to cover the V-neckline made by the points of the collar. Sew or tack the striped piece in position on the pyjama top then sew snap fasteners to each of the collar points and to the marked position on the front of the pyjama top.

Make a bow from the ribbon and fix this to the lower point of the triangular piece with a snap fastener.

Socks and shoes

Ordinary socks and shoes or gym shoes can be worn.

Mask and paws

Materials required to fit any size
35 cm ($\frac{3}{8}$ yd) of 122 cm (48 in.) wide fawn or light brown fur fabric.
70 cm ($\frac{3}{4}$ yd) of round elastic.

To make
Make the mask and paws in exactly the same way as given for Puss in Boots with the exception of the ears. Make the ear pattern as follows: first draw out a 15 cm (6 in.) diameter circle then cut off a small section as shown in diagram 2 and discard it. Make and sew on the ears as given for Puss in Boots.

Make-up

Give Baby Bear a little black nose using a black make-up crayon then draw a black line straight down from the nose to the upper lip.

Little Bo-Peep has lost her sheep,
And can't tell where to find them;
Leave them alone, and they'll come home,
And bring their tails behind them.

❧ *Little Bo-Peep* ❧

An ordinary blouse and a straw hat if available can be used as a basis for this fancy dress, though instructions are given for making all the items of clothing. The crook is very easy to make using a length of wooden dowelling and a piece of wire coat hanger for the curved top. The wire is wrapped with strips of fabric and finally lampshade braid is glued on to give an ornamental carved effect.

Skirt

Materials required for height 142 cm (4 ft 8 in.)
1·4 m (1½ yd) of 122 cm (48 in.) wide printed curtain fabric.
A length of petersham ribbon about 2·5 cm (1 in.) wide, the child's waist measurement plus 8 cm (3 in.), for the waistband.
Velcro or hooks and eyes for the waistband fastening.

To make
Cut two 122 cm (48 in.) wide strips of fabric long enough to reach to mid-calf length on the child. There should be a strip of fabric left over which will be used for the hat ribbon. Join the strips of skirt fabric at the short edges leaving a gap at the top of one seam for the side opening. Gather up the waist edge to fit the child's waist measurement and sew it to the length of ribbon. Sew *Velcro* or hooks and eyes to the waistband overlap. Hem the lower edge.

Underskirt

To make the skirt stand out well, an underskirt can be made in the same way as the skirt from old cotton sheeting. Gather the waist edge on to a length of tape, leaving enough tape at each end for tying around the waist.

Blouse

Note that this blouse should fit any size without adjustment because of the elasticated neck edge and sleeves.

Materials
1·4 m (1½ yd) of 92 cm (36 in.) wide fabric.
1·9 m (2 yd) of narrow elastic.

To make
Use the tunic pattern given on page 10. Shorten the lower edge to the line marked A, then lengthen the sleeve edges so that they reach to the child's wrists. Cut the neck edge along the line marked A. Cut the blouse from fabric as shown in diagram 1. Stitch two strips of elastic to each sleeve parallel with the wrist edges, spacing them out as shown in diagram 1. The elastic should be firmly stretched as it is being stitched on so that it will tightly gather up the fabric.

Hem the wrist edges of the sleeves, then join the side and underarm seams. Clip the underarm curves. Hem the lower and neck edges of the blouse forming casings for the elastic and clipping the neck edge if necessary. Thread elastic through to fit the neck and waist loosely. The blouse should be worn outside the skirt.

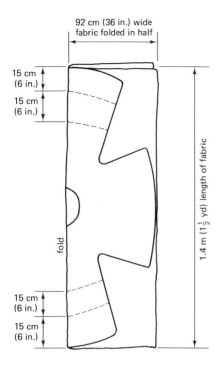

92 cm (36 in.) wide
fabric folded in half

15 cm
(6 in.)

15 cm
(6 in.)

fold

1.4 m (1½ yd) length of fabric

15 cm
(6 in.)

15 cm
(6 in.)

1 Cutting out the blouse

2 Sewing the straps
in place

Bodice and overskirt

Materials required for height 142 cm (4 ft 8 in.)
92 cm (1 yd) of 92 cm (36 in.) wide non-woven curtain fabric.
23 cm (¼ yd) of 82 cm (32 in.) wide stiff interlining.
Metal eyelets if available.
92 cm (1 yd) of narrow braid for lacing up the bodice front.
2·1 m (2¼ yd) of braid or ric-rac for edging the bodice.
Contact adhesive.

To make
For the bodice cut a 20·5 cm (8 in.) wide strip of interlining long enough to go around the child's chest leaving a gap of about 5 cm (2 in.) at the centre front. Mark the positions of the underarms then cut out two shallow semi-circles at the marked underarm positions. Spread glue all round the edges of the bodice and place it on a piece of the curtain fabric then cut out the fabric even with the interlining shape. For

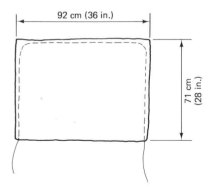

92 cm (36 in.)

71 cm
(28 in.)

3 Gathering three edges
to fit the lower edge
of the bodice

72

each shoulder strap cut a 4 cm × 25·5 cm (1½ in. × 10 in.) strip of interlining, then glue them to the curtain fabric and cut out. Taking very narrow seams, sew the ends of the straps to the front and back of the bodice as shown in diagram 2.

Stitch braid to all the raw edges of the bodice except the lower edge. Fix eyelets at even intervals for the lace holes down the front edges of the bodice, or make small holes and seal the raw edges by spreading on a little glue and allowing it to dry.

For the overskirt use the remaining piece of curtain fabric measuring 71 cm × 92 cm (28 in. × 36 in.). Gather up the piece around three edges to fit the lower edge of the bodice, leaving one 92 cm (36 in.) edge ungathered as shown in diagram 3. Sew the gathered edge to the lower edge of the bodice. When the over-skirt is worn, the ungathered 92 cm (36 in.) raw edge is tucked to the inside. Lace up the bodice with the length of braid.

Straw hat

Materials required to fit all sizes
46 cm (½ yd) of 122 cm (48 in.) wide fawn curtain fabric which should be coarsely woven to resemble straw.
46 cm (½ yd) of 82 cm (32 in.) wide stiff interlining.
1·4 m (1½ yd) of braid.
Contact adhesive.

To make
For the hat shape cut two 40·5 cm (16 in.) diameter circles of interlining and glue them together round the edges. Make a cut from the outer edge to the centre of the circle, then overlap and glue these cut edges about 10 cm (4 in.) at the outer edge to form a cone shape.

To cover the outside of the hat cut a 46 cm (18 in.) square of the curtain fabric, spread glue round the edge of the hat shape and also the point, then place the fabric over the shape. Gently pull and stretch the fabric to fit the shape smoothly. Trim the edges of the fabric even with the edge of the hat shape. Cover the inside of the hat in the same way but leave about 1·3 cm ($\frac{1}{2}$ in.) of fabric all round when trimming the edges. Turn and glue the 1·3 cm ($\frac{1}{2}$ in.) extra on to the outside of the hat then glue on braid to cover the raw edge.

Use the remaining strip of skirt fabric for the ribbon. Hem the edges, then tie it round the hat as illustrated. Sew the ribbon to the hat to hold it in position.

The crook

Materials
A 122 cm (4 ft) length of 1·3 cm ($\frac{1}{2}$ in.) diameter wooden dowelling.
A wire coat hanger.
1·4 m (1$\frac{1}{2}$ yd) of lampshade braid in a fawn shade to match the wooden dowelling.
70 cm ($\frac{3}{4}$ yd) of ribbon for the bow.
Sticky tape.
Oddment of cotton fabric for padding the wire.
Impact adhesive.

To make
Cut a 40·5 cm (16 in.) length of wire off the coat hanger and bend it to the shape shown in diagram 4. A smooth curve can be obtained by bending the wire around a jar or cup of suitable size. Attach the lower 8 cm (3 in.) of the wire to the dowelling by binding it in place with sticky tape to hold it firmly in position. Now pad the wire above the dowelling to the same size as the dowelling by binding the wire round and round with 2·5 cm (1 in.) wide strips of fabric.

Taper the thickness slightly towards the end of the crook and hold the beginnings and ends of the fabric strips in place with dabs of glue. Glue on the braid, winding it round and round to cover the fabric and starting below where the wire is attached to the dowelling.

Cut the opposite end of the dowelling to make the crook a suitable length for the child as shown in the illustration. Tie the ribbon to the crook in a bow, as illustrated.

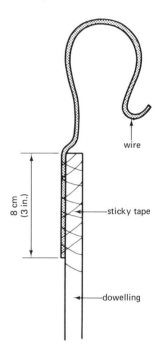

4 Bending and attaching the wire to the dowelling

When Aladdin rubbed the old lamp a very strange
and wonderful thing happened

✿ *Aladdin* ✿

This is a suitable fancy dress for a boy or girl using an ordinary pair of pyjamas as a basis. The magic lamp can be made from an old gravy or sauce boat.

Shirt and pants

For these use a pair of pyjamas, if possible a size or two larger than the child would normally wear so that the legs of the pants will hang in baggy folds around the ankles. Run a tacking thread along the inside of each of the pyjama sleeves parallel with the seams to make the sleeves fit tightly to the wrists. The tacking threads can be removed later. The pyjama top should be worn back to front.

Shoes

Use black slip-on gym shoes, gluing a strip of 2 cm ($\frac{3}{4}$ in.) wide white elastic round the soles as shown in the illustration.

Wig

Materials required to fit any size
A piece of black knitted-type fabric, for example black brushed nylon or wool jersey, measuring 30·5 cm × 61 cm (12 in. × 24 in.).
Short length of narrow elastic.

To make
Cut an 18 cm (7 in.) wide strip of the fabric long enough to go around the child's head plus 2·5 cm (1 in.). Run a gathering thread along the centre of the strip parallel to the short edges,

pull up the gathers to measure 9 cm (3½ in.) and fasten off. This forms the centre parting on the wig. Join the 18 cm (7 in.) edges. Hem the remaining raw edges and thread the elastic through one hem to gather up the fabric for the crown of the head.

For the plait, cut three long strips of fabric from the remaining piece and plait them together, cutting the ends to points to taper the plait towards its end. Tie black thread round the end of the plait. Sew the top end of the plait to the centre back of the wig.

When the wig is worn, tuck the child's own hair out of sight beneath it.

Tunic and hat

Materials required for height 142 cm (4 ft 8 in.)
1·9 m (2 yd) of 122 cm (48 in.) wide brocade curtain fabric.
2·5 m (2¾ yd) of braid for trimming the tunic.
Piece of stiff card for the hat shape 40·5 cm (16 in.) square.
Sticky tape.
46 cm (½ yd) of narrow black elastic for the hat.
92 cm (1 yd) of bobble braid for trimming the hat.
Contact adhesive.

To make the tunic
Use the tunic pattern as given on page 10. Try the pattern against the child to check that the lower edge is mid-thigh length and shorten or lengthen the pattern as necessary. Cut out the tunic from fabric, then cut out the V-neckline on the front only.

Join the underarm and side seams from the wrist edges only as far as the line marked A on the pattern in order to leave side slits. Clip the underarm curves. Try the tunic on the child to see if larger turnings need to be taken on these

seams and also to check if the sleeve edges need to be shortened.

Turn the raw wrist and neck edges 0·6 cm (¼ in.) to the outside and stitch down, clipping the neck edge if necessary. Hem the lower edges and the side slits.

Stitch braid to the wrist edges to cover the raw edges of the tunic. Stitch braid around the neck edge, across to one side seam then down the side seam to the hem, easing the braid in to tucks around the curved neck edge to make it fit.

To make the hat
Make the basic hat shape from card using three-quarters of a 40·5 cm (16 in.) diameter circle as a pattern. Overlap the straight edges of the card about 5 cm (2 in.) at the outer edge, tapering up to the point. Hold this edge firmly in place with sticky tape.

Cut two pieces of brocade fabric using the basic three-quarter circle pattern, allowing 1·3 cm (½ in.) extra on the straight edges for seams and also 1·3 cm (½ in.) extra on the outer edges. Place the wrong side of one fabric shape on the outside of the hat and pin the straight edges together to make the fabric fit the hat smoothly. Sew the seam as pinned, trim the seam, then glue the wrong side of the fabric piece to the inside of the hat.

Pierce a hole for the elastic in each side of the hat about 10 cm (4 in.) down from the top point. Push the ends of the elastic through the holes to the outside of the hat and glue down the ends, adjusting the length of the elastic to suit the child.

Cover the outside of the hat with fabric in the same way as for the inside. Trim the remaining raw edges of the fabric even with the card then glue on the bobble braid as illustrated.

The magic lamp

Materials

An old gravy or sauce boat.
Bits of braid, paper doyleys and a bottle cap for decorating the lamp.
Piece of thin card for covering the top of the lamp.
Gold and black enamel paint.
Contact adhesive.

To make

Cut a piece of card to cover in the top of the gravy boat leaving a rounded hole at the spout end. Glue the card in position then cover the join by gluing braid all round the top, round the spout and down the handle. Decorate the lamp by gluing on bits of paper doyley, strips of braid and a bottle cap to the top as illustrated.

Paint the entire lamp with gold enamel paint and leave to dry. To give an antique finish, go over the decorated parts of the lamp with black enamel paint. When this is dry, lightly brush over the black parts once more using gold paint.

Make-up

Use a black eyeliner pencil to give Aladdin's eyes and eyebrows a slant-eyed look.

Mary, Mary, quite contrary,
How does your garden grow?
With silver bells and cockle shells,
And pretty maids all in a row.

Mary, Mary, quite contrary

This outfit is made from pink cotton gingham fabric. The posy has small silver bells and cockle shells glued on to it. The 'pretty maids' in the rhyme could be portrayed by a few smaller children dressed in the same way as Mary but in a different colour.

Dress and hat

Materials required for height 142 cm (4 ft 8 in.)
2·8 m (3 yd) of 92 cm (36 in.) wide fabric.
6·4 m (7 yd) of lace edging for trimming the edges of the dress and hat.
23 cm ($\frac{1}{4}$ yd) of 92 cm (36 in.) wide plain taffeta for the belt.
8 cm (3 in.) of *Velcro* or hooks and eyes for the belt fastening.
1·6 m (1$\frac{3}{4}$ yd) of narrow elastic.

To make the dress
Use the tunic pattern given on page 10 altering it as follows: shorten the sleeve edges to the lines marked A, then cut out the neck edge along the line marked A. Lengthen the hem edge of the tunic to make it about 30·5 cm (12 in.) above floor level when tried against the child. There is no need to alter the width of the pattern because the elasticated waist and sleeves ensure that the dress will fit all sizes.

Cut out the tunic shape and all the other pieces for the hat and frills, etc as shown in diagram 1. Hem the sleeve edges then stitch on lace edging. Stitch a 20·5 cm (8 in.) length of elastic to the wrong side of each sleeve about 5 cm (2 in.) from the sleeve edges, stretching the elastic to fit as it is sewn on. Stitch two

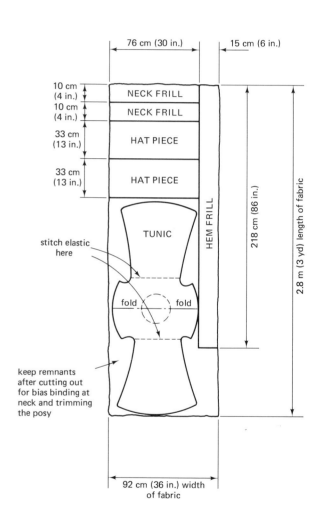

Cutting out the dress and hat pieces

30·5 cm (12 in.) lengths of elastic to the wrong side of the tunic almost level with the armholes as shown in diagram 1, stretching the elastic to fit as for the sleeves. Gather up the raw neck edge to measure 61 cm (24 in.) all round.

Join the side and underarm seams and clip the underarm curves. Join the short edges of the hem frill, then hem one long raw edge and stitch on lace edging. Gather up the other long raw edge to fit the lower edge of the tunic and stitch it in place. Join the short edges of the neck frill pieces, then hem and sew lace edging to one long raw edge. Gather up the other raw edge to fit the gathered neckline. Sew the frill to the neck edge with the raw edges even. Cut bias strips of fabric from remnants of the dress fabric and bind the raw neck edges.

For the belt cut a 10 cm (4 in.) wide strip of taffeta long enough to go around the child's waist plus 8 cm (3 in.) for the back overlap. Narrowly hem all the raw edges then press the strip into pleats along the length. Sew *Velcro* or hooks and eyes to the back edges then make a bow with the remaining piece of taffeta having first hemmed all the raw edges. Sew the bow to one back edge of the belt.

To hold the belt in position make belt carriers from loops of sewing thread just under the arms of the dress.

To make the hat
Join the two hat pieces together at two of the 33 cm (13 in.) edges. Hem and sew lace edging to one of the long edges. To the wrong side of the strip, stitch a 46 cm (18 in.) length of elastic parallel to and 10 cm (4 in.) from the lace

trimmed edge, stretching the elastic to fit as it is sewn in place. Join the remaining short raw edges of the strip. Turn in the remaining long raw edge 0·6 cm ($\frac{1}{4}$ in.) and gather it up as tightly as possible then fasten off the gathering thread.

The posy

Materials
Remnants of the dress fabric.
Small piece of card.
Scraps of green felt.
A few cockle shells.
A few silver bells.
Contact adhesive.

To make
Cut a 13 cm (5 in.) diameter circle of card and glue green felt to one side. On to the green felt glue cockle shells, bells and green felt cut into leaf shapes. To the back of the posy glue a tube of card covered with fabric for a handle, then glue a frill made from remnants of dress fabric round the edge of the posy.

Shoes, socks and gloves

Ballet shoes or slippers can be worn, sewing a small rosette of fabric to the fronts as illustrated. The socks and gloves are white.

Watering can

A plastic toy watering can completes the outfit.

. . . and Puss in Boots entered the Ogre's fine castle

Puss in Boots

Puss wears a dashing Cavalier style outfit. This costume is best suited to small children and can be worn by a boy or girl. While a pair of ordinary trousers or pyjama pants can be used, the pants illustrated are easy to make using striped curtain fabric.

Mask, paws and tail

Materials required to fit any size
35 cm (⅜ yd) of 122 cm (48 in.) wide black fur fabric.
70 cm (¾ yd) of black, round elastic.

To make
For the mask cut two 25·5 cm × 28 cm (10 in. × 11 in.) pieces of fur fabric. On one piece cut out the holes for the mouth and eyes at the positions shown in diagram 1. Now join the two pieces of fur fabric round three edges taking 0·6 cm (¼ in.) seam, leaving the lower 28 cm (11 in.) edges open and rounding off the upper corners as shown in the diagram. Trim off the excess fabric at the corners and turn right side out. Run a 30·5 cm (12 in.) length of elastic round the lower edge and knot the ends together.

Cut out four ear pieces to the size shown in the diagram. Join them in pairs taking 0·6 cm (¼ in.) seam and leaving the lower 10 cm (4 in.) edges open. Turn the ears right side out and oversew the raw edges together, pulling the stitches tightly to gather slightly. Sew the gathered edges of the ears in position as shown in the diagram.

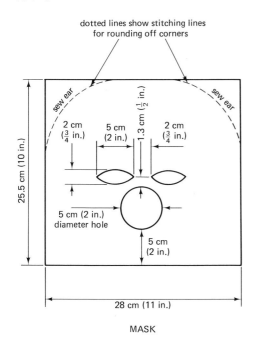

MASK

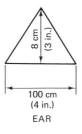

EAR

Patterns for mask

For each paw, cut two 10 cm × 20·5 cm (4 in. × 8 in.) strips of fur fabric. Join them in pairs taking 0·6 cm (¼ in.) seam, leaving one 10 cm (4 in.) edge open in each pair and rounding off all other corners. Trim off the corners and turn the paws right side out. Make two loops from the round elastic and wear these on the wrists on top of the paws to hold them in position.

For the tail cut a 6·5 cm × 33 cm (2½ in. × 13 in.) strip of fur fabric and cut the strip to a point at one end for the end of the tail. Oversew the long edges together with the right side of the fabric outside.

Pants

Materials required to fit any size
92 cm (1 yd) of 122 cm (48 in.) wide striped curtain fabric.
70 cm (¾ yd) of 2·5 cm (1 in.) wide elastic.

To make
Cut out and make the pants as in the instructions on page 12. Sew the top end of the tail to the back of the pants about 20·5 cm (8 in.) down from the waist edge.

Lacy shirt

Trim a white school shirt or blouse with gathered ruffles of lace trimming tacked to the collar, cuffs and down the centre front. As an economical substitute for lace trimming, 23 cm (¼ yd) of lacy curtain net cut into strips and gathered will do very well.

Boots

Black wellington boots are used, making the turn-over tops from leatherette or felt.

Materials
A piece of black leatherette or felt 35.5 cm (14 in.) square.
Contact adhesive or a rubberised adhesive if the tops are to be removed later.

To make
For the turn-over tops make a paper pattern as follows: draw out a 35·5 cm (14 in.) diameter circle, cut it out, then draw an 18 cm (7 in.) diameter circle in the centre of the 35·5 cm (14 in.) diameter circle, cut it out and discard it. Cut the remaining pattern piece in half and using one half as a pattern, cut out two pieces from leatherette or felt.

Fit the inner curved edge of each piece about 1·3 cm (½ in.) inside the top edge of each boot, overlapping and pinning the short straight edges together at the backs of the boots as necessary to fit. Remove the tops, then sew the overlapped edges together as pinned, cutting off any excess. Glue the inner curved edges 1·3 cm (½ in.) inside the tops of the boots.

Cape

Materials required to fit any size
1·2 m (1¼ yd) of 122 cm (48 in.) wide curtain fabric.
4·6 m (5 yd) of narrow braid or bias binding.

To make
Make a paper pattern for the cape as follows: draw and cut out a 112 cm (44 in.) diameter circle with a 13 cm (5 in.) diameter circle cut out of the centre for the neck edge. Cut away one quarter of the circle altogether and discard it. Use the remaining three-quarter circle as a pattern.

Cut out the cape and either bind the raw edges with bias binding or turn and press them

0·6 cm (¼ in.) to the outside of the cape, clipping the neck curve, and stitch on braid to cover the raw edges. When binding the neck edge leave lengths of braid or bias at the centre front neck edges to use as ties.

Hat

Materials required to fit any size
46 cm (½ yd) of 122 cm (48 in.) wide plain fabric.
A 40·5 cm (16 in.) square of stiff interlining.
1·4 m (1½ yd) of bias binding.
A few large feathers or bits of marabou feather trimming.
Contact adhesive.

To make
For the hat brim cut a 40·5 cm (16 in.) diameter circle from the square of interlining. Cut out a 16·5 cm (6½ in.) diameter circle from the centre and discard it. Spread a little glue round the outer and inner edge of the brim shape and then stick it on to the hat fabric. Cut out the brim even with the interlining shape at the centre and outer edges. Cover the other side of the interlining with fabric in the same way. Bind the outer edge of the brim with bias binding.

For the crown of the hat cut two 18 cm × 29 cm (7 in. × 11½ in.) strips of hat fabric. Join these pieces together at the 18 cm (7 in.) edges taking 0·6 cm (¼ in.) seams. Now stitch one of the long raw edges of the crown to the centre edge of the brim taking 0·6 cm (¼ in.) seam. Trim the seam. Run a gathering thread along the remaining raw edge of the crown, pull up the gathers tightly and fasten off the thread.

Sew feathers to the hat brim as illustrated.

Belt

Any available belt can be used, or a belt can be made from a strip of leather cloth, attaching a buckle to one end.

Rapier or sword

A cheap plastic toy sword tucked in to the belt completes the outfit.

✺ *Some other suggestions* ✺

Snow-White

Skirt, as for Bo-Peep using plain fabric with bands of coloured braid sewn round the lower edge.

Blouse, as for Bo-Peep threading elastic through the wrist and neck edges only.

Bodice, as for Bo-Peep making it from black fabric or felt and omitting the overskirt.

Dwarf

Suitable for a very small child if appearing with a tall child as Snow-White.

Tights, sweater, tunic, boots and belt as for Robin Hood using bright colours.

Collar, as for Friar Tuck.

Cap, made the same shape as Willie Winkie's.

Beard, use a strip of shaggy long pile fur fabric to go around the lower edge of the face, attaching each end to the ears with loops of elastic.

Hair, to match the beard, sew a strip of fur fabric to the inside of the lower edge of the cap.

Prince

Tights, sweater, tunic and collar as for the Knave of Hearts, using brocade fabrics decorated with braid. A strip of contrasting coloured fabric can be gathered along one edge and sewn to the straight back edge of the collar to hang down for a cloak effect.

Sleeves, as for the Queen of Hearts, attaching them to the sweater armholes at the upper edges and gathering in at the wrist edges.

Crown, as for the Queen of Hearts, covering it in gold or silver fabric or paper, and edging it with braid. Coloured transparent fruit sweets can be glued on for jewels.

Little Boy Blue

Pants, socks and shoes as for Hot Cross Buns.

Shirt, as for Hot Cross Buns but leave it long enough to be worn as a smock outside the trousers. Work cross stitches or sew braid across the front and back at chest height for a 'smocked' effect.

Cap, as for Hot Cross Buns but shorten the brim to measure only 5 cm or 8 cm (2 in. or 3 in.) and gather a smaller circle of fabric to the top for the crown of the cap.

Horn, use a toy horn or make a cone-shaped horn from a piece of card.

Jack and Jill

Suitable for a small boy and girl.

For Jack, pants, socks and shoes as for Hot Cross Buns. Use an ordinary shirt.

Hat as for Little Boy Blue.

Jacket, make in the same way as for Goldilocks.

For Jill, make outfit as for Little Red Riding Hood, omitting the hood and instead making a bonnet as for Goldilocks.

A small pail can be carried between the children.

Dick Whittington

Sweater, tights, tunic and belt as for Robin Hood, using plain fabrics in dull colours.
Boots, as for Puss in Boots.
Cap, make the brim the same shape as for the Knave of Hearts' crown, then for the centre of the cap sew on a gathered circle of fabric to the lower edge of the brim. Sew a feather to the cap.
Tie a red handkerchief bundle to the end of a rough stick for Dick to carry on his shoulder.

Old King Cole

Make as for the Prince's outfit using bright contrasting colours.
Make the extra sleeves elbow length only and gather them in to the elbows.
Use white long pile fur fabric to make a beard and hair as given for the Dwarf. Make a crown as given for Dick Whittington's cap.
Tie a ribbon bow round each leg just below the knee.
King Cole can carry a clay pipe and a bowl.

The little match girl

Make a ragged outfit similar to Cinderella's, using dull colours.
Use a rough square of fabric frayed and torn for wearing on the head as a shawl.
From a grocery box make a little tray with a few matches on it made from thin bits of wood with red sealing wax blobs on the end.

Pat-a-cake, pat-a-cake, baker's man

Make an outfit as for Hot Cross Buns.
Instead of the tray of buns make a cake from a round container such as shallow cake tin. Glue a circle of white card to the tin for the icing sugar top of the cake and cover the sides of the cake with a cake frill. For piped icing sugar decoration use silky cord glued to the cake top in patterns then glue a letter 'B' made from cord to the centre of the cake.